Cover: Menomini Indians painted from life. S.M. Brookes, 1858, Milwaukee Public Museum collections.

THE WOODLAND INDIANS

of the Western Great Lakes

Robert E. Ritzenthaler
and
Pat Ritzenthaler

WAVELAND

PRESS, INC.

Prospect Heights, Illinois

For information about this book, write or call:

    Waveland Press, Inc.
    P.O. Box 400
    Prospect Heights, Illinois 60070
    (847) 634-0081

Unless otherwise acknowledged, all photographs for this book have been provided by the Milwaukee Public Museum.

ISBN 0-88133-548-7

Printed in the United States of America

7

Contents

Dedication

Robert E. Ritzenthaler was born in Milwaukee in 1911. He received his undergraduate degrees from the University of Wisconsin and his Ph.D. from Columbia University. In 1938 Dr. Ritzenthaler joined the Anthropology Department at the Milwaukee Public Museum, eventually becoming Head Curator. Because his work at the museum covered so many cultures of the world, he found it a joy as well as a duty to do ethnological field work among the Oneida, Chippewa, and Potawatomi Indians of Wisconsin, the Kickapoo Indians in northern Mexico, the Caroline Islands in Micronesia, and the Cameroons in West Africa. He participated in archaeological excavations in Wisconsin, Illinois, and Guatemala. He was a staff lecturer in anthropology at the University of Wisconsin - Milwaukee and, for many years, before his retirement in 1972, was editor of *The Wisconsin Archaeologist.*

Pat Ritzenthaler is a graduate of DePauw University in Indiana. She has made frequent excursions among the Woodland Indians and a lengthy field trip to the Cameroons. As a result of the African trip, Mrs. Ritzenthaler wrote *The Fon of Bafut,* a biographical study of the chief of the Bafut people. She has also written numerous articles for children on American Indian life.

When Dr. Ritzenthaler died in 1980, he had written numerous articles about the Woodland Indians and contributed to the *Handbook of Northern American Indians,* published by the Smithsonian Institution, (1978). The Woodland Indians were undoubtedly the people who "turned him on" to ethnology, and he had many friends among them.

It is with sincere thanks to the Milwaukee Public Museum that this second printing is dedicated.

Pat Ritzenthaler

Milwaukee, 1983

Preface

The Woodland Indians have never caught the fancy of the world as have some of the other American Indians. It is true that they were introduced, to some extent, through Longfellow's poem *Hiawatha,* the works of James Fenimore Cooper, and the story of Pocahontas; and the historically minded are familiar with such prominent Woodland Indian names as King Philip, Black Hawk, and Chief Pontiac. This indifference may be due, perhaps, to the paucity of colorful Woodland Indian figures, as compared to the number of charismatic men who came out of the Plains and Southwest—men like Sitting Bull, Geronimo, Cochise, and Crazy Horse. It may be due to the fact that Woodland ceremonies are not as dramatic as the Sun Dance of the Plains Indians or the Snake Dance of the Hopi. Nor have Woodland craft products stimulated collectors of primitive art as have the Navahos' blankets and silverwork, the Northwest Coast aborigines' wood carving, or the pottery of the Pueblos. Part of it must lie in the fact that relatively few books have been written for a popular audience, books that would acquaint the man on the street with some of the interesting aspects of life that do exist in Woodland culture.

That the Woodland Indian culture, however, was not without its own form of color, drama, and ingenuity will be demonstrated here by word and picture. Much of the story was compiled from the studies of such pioneer ethnologists as Frances Densmore, Walter Hoffman, and Alanson Skinner. Some information and, I hope, flavor are derived from my own field work, which encompasses a period of nearly thirty years. While the bulk of my time was spent among the Wisconsin Chippewa, I also was fortunate in staying with the Potawatomi, Kickapoo, and Oneida, and I made briefer visits to the Winnebago and Menomini. It is with a certain nostalgia that I look back over the many hours spent in their company recording data, attending religious ceremonies, funerals, and social events, and just sheer visiting. I remember the fun times of playing cribbage with the Chippewa (who taught me the game), fishing with them in their favorite spots, and camping with them in the wild rice fields. With the exception of the Mexican Kickapoo, I encountered hospitality among them all, with friendliness, courtesy, and co-operation beyond reasonable expectation. In some manner, perhaps, this volume will repay my Indian friends for the patient investment of their time in my work.

I am deeply indebted to Victor Barnouw, John Dowling, Nancy O. Lurie, and Steven Polyak for reading parts of the manuscript and making valuable suggestions and criticisms. The photographs, except where otherwise noted, are reproduced through the courtesy of the Milwaukee Public Museum.

Robert E. Ritzenthaler

Milwaukee, 1969

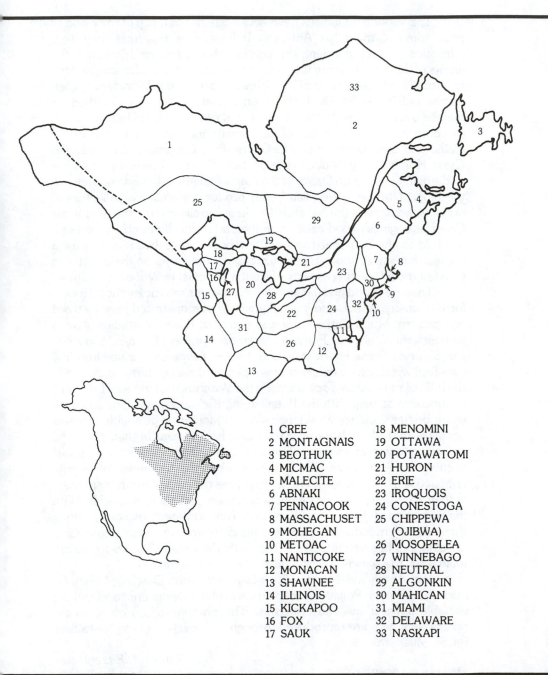

1 CREE
2 MONTAGNAIS
3 BEOTHUK
4 MICMAC
5 MALECITE
6 ABNAKI
7 PENNACOOK
8 MASSACHUSET
9 MOHEGAN
10 METOAC
11 NANTICOKE
12 MONACAN
13 SHAWNEE
14 ILLINOIS
15 KICKAPOO
16 FOX
17 SAUK

18 MENOMINI
19 OTTAWA
20 POTAWATOMI
21 HURON
22 ERIE
23 IROQUOIS
24 CONESTOGA
25 CHIPPEWA
   (OJIBWA)
26 MOSOPELEA
27 WINNEBAGO
28 NEUTRAL
29 ALGONKIN
30 MAHICAN
31 MIAMI
32 DELAWARE
33 NASKAPI

1

The Forest and the Prairie

The Woodland Indians, at the time of Columbus' arrival in the New World, occupied the forested area of eastern North America. This huge geographical area, in which most of the tribes shared a similar language and culture, is the largest of the eight culture areas into which the Indians of North America have been grouped. It extends from the Mississippi River eastward to the Atlantic Coast, and, roughly, from a line north of what is now Tennessee into most of the eastern half of Canada.

Eastward from Lake Superior to the New England states there was a broad belt of mixed deciduous and coniferous trees. North of this belt the trees were primarily coniferous and south of it mostly deciduous (Farb, 1963). In the belt stretching from Illinois through Ohio to southern New England were oaks and hickory, while patches of prairie lands were found in the western section. North of this belt, banding across the country from northern Wisconsin to New York, was the "northern hardwood forest," made up of birch, beech, and maple, with inclusions of basswood, elm, and ash. The Woodland Indians were extremely knowledgeable concerning the properties and uses of trees and other plants, and they exploited that knowledge to the fullest. Such wild foods as wild rice, nuts, berries, and fruits were an essential part of their diet. A great variety of medicines were concocted from the flora, some of them being used today in our own materia medica. Wood, bark, and plant fibers were valuable for the arts and artifacts of material culture. The paper birch was especially useful for the Indians' wigwams, canoes, and food and storage containers, while the maple was utilized for its sugar. Stone, bone, and hides also provided utilitarian material.

The area occupied by these Indians offered few natural barriers. The Appalachian Mountains and the five Great Lakes restricted movement to some extent, but the Great Lakes were also avenues for shore-line water traffic. The climate was characterized by the four seasons, with considerable extremes in temperature between winter and summer. Agriculture or gardening was generally practiced, but climatic conditions among the northerly, subarctic tribes, such as the Naskapi and the Montagnais,

11

precluded the growth of crops. In these areas, heavy snowfalls sometimes measured up to eighty inches a year and made snowshoes a necessity for winter travel. Where it was possible to do so, the people raised corn, beans, and squash, but their economy was based almost entirely on the exploitation of wild resources. Survival depended on their knowledge of these resources, and, although it was not always an easy life, they were able to live in their environment.

The Algonkian-speaking peoples were the first Indians encountered by the white settlers of the United States; indeed, there were some thirty major tribes that spoke Algonkian languages, nine that spoke Iroquoian, and a few, such as the Winnebago and the Santee Sioux, that spoke Siouan. The meetings, for the most part, were amicable, and the friendly Indians taught the white man much about their environment. The settlers learned about such useful crops as corn, squash, and pumpkins; they observed new planting and cooking techniques and were introduced to the practice of smoking tobacco. The English-American vocabulary has been enriched by such Algonkian words as moose, muskellunge, succotash, hominy, squash, wigwam, papoose, squaw, papaw, tomahawk, and others. Twenty-four American states bear Indian names, and many of those east of the Mississippi River were Algonkian in origin: Massachusetts, Connecticut, Wisconsin, Illinois, and others. The names of many cities, Chicago and Milwaukee for instance, were derived from members of this linguistic family, as were those of various rivers and lakes: Mississippi, Michigan, Ontario. In some areas the white settlers found certain items of Indian ingenuity as useful enough to adapt for their own use: the birchbark canoes and moccasins are good examples. The basic form of the Chippewa canoe is still apparent in our modern canoes, and the Iroquoian-style moccasin (an Algonkian word) is found in any shoe store today.

Having been the first to greet the white man, these Indians were also the first to disappear, leaving the eastern half of the United States few remnants of their former population, which, at the time of contact, was estimated at about two hundred thousand. War and new diseases eliminated many of them. Others intermarried with the whites, and they, as well as their descendants, merged further into the general population until traces of their Indianness became invisible. Perhaps the most important cause of their numerical decline was the United States' removal policy, begun in the early nineteenth century and devised in order to shift all Indians east of the Mississippi to a region known as Indian Territory. Testimony of its success is the fact that this area, now known as Oklahoma, contains not only the greatest numbers of remnant Woodland tribes, but nearly one third of all Indians in the United States; for, of the some six hundred thousand Indians today, less than ten percent are found in the area east of the Mississippi River. The tribes of the western Great Lakes region comprised the largest population of any of the divisions of the Woodland area, although even here the population was not dense nor the tribes large. While the largest tribe, the Chippewa (Ojibwa), now consists of United States bands numbering some thirty thousand, with another fifty thousand in Canada, the majority of the Central Algonkian tribes numbered only a few thousand at the time of contact.

In an area as large as the Woodland there were, of course, regional variations in culture. The Algonkian-speaking tribes can be grouped into these main divisions: the Central Algonkians, the Eastern Algonkians, and the Subarctic Algonkians. The Iroquoian-speaking tribes made up a fourth group for the area. These four groups can be further divided into the following sub-groups:

Estimated Population at the Time of Columbus (Mooney, 1928)

I. Central Algonkian

Forest Tribes

Chippewa 50,000   Menomini 3,000
Ottawa 4,000   Cree 20,000
Potawatomi 4,000

Prairie Tribes

Sauk 3,000   Shawnee 3,000
Fox 3,000   Piankashaw 1,000
Kickapoo 2,000   Prairie Potawatomi 4,000
Miami 4,500   (Mascouten)
Peoria)
Illinois) 8,000   Winnebago 3,800

II. Eastern Algonkian/ United States

Micmac 3,500   Montauk 6,000
Malecite 800   Abnaki 3,800
Pennacook 2,000   Narraganset 5,000
Mahican 3,000   Wampanoag 3,000
Pequot 2,200   Delaware 8,000
Massachuset 13,000

III. Subarctic Algonkian/Eastern Canada

Montagnais 2,000
Naskapi 2,000

IV. Iroquois

Seneca)		Huron/Wyandot 10,000
Onondaga)		Erie 4,000
Mohawk)	20,000	Susquehanna 3,000
Oneida)		Conestoga 5,000
Cayuga)		Neutral 10,000

Of these four divisions, the Iroquois were the most divergent. Their language was not Algonkian, they practiced intensive agriculture rather than gardening, their ceremonial life was unlike the others', their clans were matrilineal (while those of the Algonkian tribes were patrilineal), and, also unlike the other tribes, they lived in multifamily long houses. In material culture, however, they shared many similarities with the other Woodland tribes. Such differences as their use of stockaded villages, the blowgun, and certain ceremonial practices suggest that they may have moved into the area from the southeast, although archaeological evidence of the moment does not bear this out. They represent a distinct subculture, but space precludes a separate treatment of them here. The Canadian, or subarctic, Algonkians were also a somewhat culturally divergent group of tribes due, at least partially, to a differing and rather inhospitable ecological setting. Roaming the northern forests and barren wastes of what is now Quebec and Newfoundland, tribes like the Naskapi and the Montagnais eked out a precarious existence mainly by hunting caribou, although deer, elk, small game, fish, and game birds were also important items of the food quest. In place of the dome-shaped wigwam so widely used by other Algonkian peoples, these tribes lived in caribou-skin-covered, conical tipis. Their tools and utensils were relatively crude, except for their snowshoes, which were beautifully designed and constructed, and generally are considered to be the finest made by any of the American Indians. Because of their position as a peripheral group, the Canadian Algonkians will be eliminated from further discussion. Likewise, the Eastern Algonkians will be mentioned but briefly, although they must be considered as typical of the general Woodland pattern. The chief difficulty in discussing these tribes of the northeastern seaboard is that they were the first to have contact with the whites and were the first to lose their traditional culture. The result has been a lack of good descriptive accounts. It is known that they were generally similar to the Central Algonkians in their material culture, economic life, and religious concepts. While the Central Algonkians remained discrete tribal units, the chief difference was in terms of political structure. By the early historic period, the numerous tiny seaboard tribes had been organized into a series of confederacies for mutual protection against the colonists and the Iroquois. During the seventeenth century most of these were disrupted as a result of wars with the colonists. For example, confederacies such as that of the Wampanoag (which consisted of thirty villages) and the Narra-ganset (made up of eight villages) were conquered and split up by the whites during King Philip's War of 1675-76.

Although we will concentrate mainly on the Central Algonkians of the western Great Lakes area, subdivision is apparent between the Forest tribes to the north and the Prairie tribes to the south. This distinction depends on the time period selected, for at one time the groups presently classified as Prairie—the Sauk, Fox, Kickapoo, and Prairie Potawatomi (Skinner adds only confusion by calling them Mascoutens)—were living in a forested or at least a semiforested environment, and presumably they adapted to it. By the eighteenth century these tribes had begun moving southward, especially from southcentral Wisconsin, into the prairies. The resulting changes were mainly in material culture. For example, the movement south of the birch line meant the loss of birch bark for contain-ers, canoes, and wigwam coverings. It also meant that certain food resources like wild rice and big game like the moose and caribou were not available. There were, however, certain advantages in the form of milder winters and a longer growing season. The variation in social organization cannot be accounted for, of course, on environmental grounds, and their dialectical similarity was the result of propinquity. The Sauk, Fox, Kicka-poo, Prairie Potawatomi, and Shawnee spoke dialects that were very closely related. The Miami and Illinois formed another dialectical block. Among the Forest tribes the closest dialectical and cultural similarities were between the Forest Potawatomi, the Ottawa, and the Chippewa—sometimes referred to as the "three fires." The Menomini were culturally similar, but dialectically different. The Winnebago were culturally diver-gent, and, as previously mentioned, spoke a language of a different family, Siouan.

Physical Type

Like other American Indians, the Woodland people reflected such Mongoloid physical traits as brownish skin color; straight, black hair; sparse facial and body hair; dark eyes; wide malars (cheekbones); a trace of the epicanthic fold, which is most apparent in infants; and the Mongo-lian spot, a bluish-black patch at the base of the spine, also observable mostly in infants.

There are few physical studies that attempt to define the Woodland type. Howells (1946, p. 168), Hrdlicka, and Dixson point out the prevailing dolichocephaly, or longheadedness, of the Indians in the New York/New England area, and they note the appearance of roundheadedness among the Iroquois and such Canadian groups as the Montagnais, Naskapi, and Beothuk. In general, however, the longheaded tendency seems to have

15

prevailed over most of the Woodland area. On the basis of personal observation, the Woodland Indians appeared to be medium to tall in height, averaging perhaps 5 feet 7 inches for the men and about 5 inches less for the women. Body build ranged from slender to medium, with obesity rather rare, although among women of middle age and older a certain stockiness was common.

Prehistory

The Woodland Indians first appeared upon the scene about the time of Christ. They seem to have been more a product of a development from existing archaic cultures than the result of a mass movement into the area. Actually, the earliest known people in the area were the Paleo-Indians who occupied most of North America, although in small hunting groups, during the end of the Pleistocene period. The earliest radiocarbon dates for the Woodland area come from the Debert site in Nova Scotia, with thirteen clustering around 8600 B.C.

Their most characteristic artifact is the fluted point, a spear point with a long groove, or flute, extending upward from the base on one or both surfaces. These people also used end scrapers, small flake knives, and engraving tools called "gravers."

Following this culture, from about 7000 B.C. to 5000 B.C., were other small groups of hunters with non-fluted points in a number of distinctive shapes and often characterized by beautiful parallel flaking. These late Paleo-Indian points, such as Scottsbluff and Eden, were named from sites on the western plains where they were found with the bones of extinct animals.

The Archaic period, from about 5000 B.C. to 1 A.D., saw another series of cultures: Old Copper, Red Ocher, and Glacial Kame, to name a few. A number of interesting developments took place among the various cultures at this time. The Old Copper people cold-hammered the native Lake Superior copper into an extensive assortment of tools and implements unmatched by later Indians. During the latter part of this period some of the finest ground stone objects were made: banner-stones, birdstones, gorgets, and tube pipes (the earliest indications of smoking). There is still no indication of agriculture at this time, but there is some evidence that mound building had begun.

By the end of the Archaic period, people had begun another phase of life, which was to be featured by mound building, pottery making, and incipient agriculture. From this time on, until the coming of the white man, the Woodland culture was found in various forms throughout the eastern half of North America, first in its prehistoric form, but with certain continuities that survived into historic times. The groups that were first seen by the white man and that are known to us today by their tribal names were derived, for the most part, from a prehistoric Woodland cultural base. While there was variation through time and from area to area, the prehistoric Woodland culture was characterized by a hunting, fishing, food-gathering economy, accompanied by limited gardening. Their chipped-stone work was rather crude, with a variety of arrowheads, scrapers, knives, and drills that utilized, primarily, percussion flaking. They also made three-quarter-grooved, ground-stone axes and elbow pipes of pottery and stone. Pottery vessels, often quite large but somewhat crude, were characterized by a grit-tempered paste and, usually, cord markings on the outer surfaces. Disposition of the dead was often by interment in relatively low earthern mounds. In the Wisconsin area one group developed the unique effigy mounds, low earthern mounds in the shapes of various birds and animals.

There are instances of historic tribes developing from a non-Woodland prehistoric base. For example, the Winnebago are known to have stemmed from an upper Mississippi culture. But, for the most part, the tribes encountered by the first Europeans could trace their immediate ancestry to people operating with one or another form of prehistoric Woodland culture.

Woman knocking rice into canoe. Chippewa.

2

The Food Quest

The food quest of the Woodland Indians was based, primarily, on hunting, fishing, and gathering wild crops. They practiced some agriculture, but it was definitely of secondary importance and consisted mostly of the Indian staples—corn, beans, and squash. Wresting a living from the forest and prairie demanded a great deal of time and effort. It necessitated considerable mobility, hence these people may be described as seminomadic. They operated out of fairly permanent villages and within a radius of perhaps a hundred miles, but their seasonal cycle kept them on the move much of the time.

Maple Sugar

In the spring, usually in March, several families would move to their sugarbush in a particular section of the maple forest, and here they would erect a wigwam and set up camp. It was a time of work but also one of pleasure. Special wigwams were retained from year to year, a small one for storing the birchbark equipment, and a larger one, in which the sap was boiled and the sugar granulated. The tree was tapped by making a horizontal gash in the trunk three or four feet above the ground. A cedar spile was pounded in at an angle, allowing the sap to drip down into a simply made birchbark bucket placed on the ground. The sap was gathered in birchbark containers and cooked by placing heated stones in them. After contact with the white man, the birchbark containers were replaced by metal kettles.

When the boiled sap hung in strings from the stirring paddle, it was considered done and was then strained through a basswood-fiber matting or through cloth, and transferred to a wooden granulating trough. Here it was worked, as it cooled, with yet another paddle as well as with the hands. The granulated sugar that resulted was pulverized into finer granules. Sometimes the sugar was packed lightly into molds, shells, bones, or carved wooden forms to make little cakes. The lighter-colored sugar was considered superior, and at times the white of an egg was added to achieve the desired color. Nothing was wasted, and if any syrup was left in the kettle, it was reboiled with a little fresh sap to make a second-grade sugar.

After all the sugar was prepared, the kettles were cleaned by a thorough scrubbing with wood ashes and a stone. The kettles and baskets were then stacked in the wigwam until the following year, and the family carried home their supply of sugar in birchbark storage containers called *makuks,* to be used when needed.

Maple sugar was used at feasts and ceremonies, and each person was expected to eat all that was set before him. The sugar was used on fruits, vegetables, cereals, and even fish. They had no salt, hence maple sugar was used as a major seasoning as well as a confection. Children were sometimes coaxed to take their medicine by putting a little maple sugar in it. The sugar was also mixed with water for a refreshing drink.

First Fruits

When the first sugar of the year was cooked, the people always offered a small amount to the Great Spirit, or *manido.* This ceremony, the Offering of the First Fruits or Game, was observed with the first preparation of each seasonal food. The *manidog* (spirits) were asked to insure good health, long life, and the safety of everyone at the feast. Small portions of the first fruits were also carried to the graves. Some Indians kept a small kettle especially for the preparation of the first fruits or first game, but this was not considered a necessity.

Agriculture

When they had gathered their maple sugar and moved to the summer grounds, the Woodland people planted small gardens nearby. The seasons were not long, but the people were able to augment their rice, meat, fish, nut, and berry diet with these garden foods.

Short wooden hoes were used. For grubbing out the roots, the men fashioned implements from the tree roots. There were also wooden implements that somewhat resembled crowbars.

The corn was generally cultivated in hills placed rather far apart, although not everyone did this. The ordinary maize was grown, and it included two kinds, an early blue form and a white form that ripened a bit later. There was also popcorn, which the Menomini called "mouse corn." Corn was boiled, roasted, and dried, to be ground later and put into stews. The Winnegabo steamed corn in an underground pit, putting in a layer of red-hot stones, a layer of husks, a layer of ripe corn, another layer of husks, and, finally, a layer of earth. Water was then poured in to help the steaming process.

Food Gathering

All through the summer and fall the women and children filled their leisure hours by gathering wild fruit, berries, and nuts. The women fastened birchbark buckets (makuks) to bands around their waists and filled them with the products of fields and bushes. At the beginning of each season, everyone was so hungry for the fresh fruits or berries that much of the crop was eaten immediately, but they gathered enough to cook, make into preserves or jams, or dry to be eaten as a seasoning with dried meat.

The Woodland area had an abundance of wild food: there were cranberries, gooseberries, June berries, blueberries, black and red raspberries; fruits included grapes, cherries, and chokecherries; nuts included acorns from the pin oak and the white oak, hickory nuts, hazelnuts, beechnuts, and butternuts; vegetables, in addition to their three favorites, included wild potatoes, wild onions, milkweed, and the root of the yellow water lily.

In August, when the plants were fully developed, special attention was given to gathering herbs for medicine. Since most varieties were in blossom at that time, it was easier to identify them, although they could be gathered at any other time—the roots in the spring and fall, and bark during the summer, "when the sap [was] in the tree." The medicine priest would offer tobacco to the four directions, as well as up and down. He put a little tobacco in the ground where he was about to dig. He then spoke in a low voice, promising that no more would be taken than was necessary, and that it was intended only for benign purposes. The plants were tied separately and dried.

Fishing

To the Woodland Indians, fishing was a year-round occupation. With plenty of streams and lakes to draw from, they depended on fish for a great part of their diet.

Among the Chippewa, says Densmore, women did most of the fishing, except for ice fishing in the winter and spear fishing in the spring. A wide variety of methods were used by nearly all the Woodland groups, including the use of fishhooks, nets, spears, traps, lures, bait, and a line for trolling.

On the large lakes, seines were used for they made it relatively easy to garner large numbers and a great variety of fish. In the old days the nets were made of bark-fiber cord and nettle-stalk twine; for many years, however, manufactured twine has been used and was even issued, relatively early, by the U.S. Government as a part of the yearly annuities. Sometimes the nets, after being thoroughly washed, were dipped in a liquid made from sumac leaves. This was to kill any odor still clinging to the cord, for the Indians said no fish would come near a net with the slightest odor on it. "Medicine" was also placed on the nets to insure a good catch.

There were two methods of spearing: one was done at night with the use of a torch (a method similar to shining deer at night) and the other in the winter through the ice. In this latter procedure a wooden lure, shaped like a minnow or a frog, was lowered through a hole in the ice. The Indian lay flat on his stomach and covered his head with a blanket, which was sometimes fashioned, over a small frame, into a miniature tent. This blocked out the light and enabled him to see the fish as it came up to strike at the lure. The Indian, holding his lure at the end of a stick, jiggled it up and down to give it a swimming motion. In his other hand he held his spear ready to strike at the proper moment.

Bait, often nothing more than a piece of old blanket, was fastened to a hook at the end of a string and then let down into the water. The hooks were usually deer bone, native copper, and, later, wire. Trolling was done from the canoe. The line was twisted around the paddler's wrist and then around the paddle itself. The action of the paddle moving through the water wiggled the line and attracted the fish.

Traps were fashioned from the twigs and branches of trees and were used for both large and small fish. The sturgeon in Lake Superior were often caught in this manner. A framework was built, in the spring, across the mouth of the river up which the fish had gone to spawn. Heavy timbers were set into the ground across the river and poles fastened to them so that the traps were heavy enough for men to sit on. The poles were connected with a basswood fiber netting. As the fish tried to return to the lake, the Indians, sitting just above the water, caught them and killed them with clubs. Another method was to build a V of rocks across a stream, with a runway at the center over which the fish would be directed and then clubbed.

The fish were cooked in a variety of ways: boiled, roasted on spits, dried on scaffolds in the sun or over a slow fire. Brook trout, and other small fish, were smoked entire. The larger fish were split and drawn, then grilled, smoked, or dried. Often the dry or smoked fish were pounded before being boiled, or pulverized and then added to corn-meal mush. Fish was added to wild rice. The roe of sturgeon was highly regarded, and it, too, was eaten fresh, or was dried for future use. In the winter, fresh fish was frozen without being cleaned. Some fish were split down the back and laid flat in a birchbark container. When they were cooked, the skin was peeled off before being eaten.

Turtles of various kinds were also eaten.

Hunting and Trapping

The food secured by hunting and trapping formed a considerable part of Woodland diet. Deer and moose were hunted, as were several kinds of fox—the red, the black, and the silver gray. Timber wolves, a large prairie wolf, and a smaller prairie wolf that was not considered very good eating, were also hunted. The bear was not killed without a special ceremony and apology, for this animal was greatly revered by the Woodland Indians.

In the old days hunting was done with chipped-stone-tipped wooden spears, and bows and arrows. Most commonly used on the hunt was the bow and arrow, its relative crudity necessitating a stalking technique and shooting at close range. After white contact, guns soon replaced the bow.

A successful hunter was one who fasted and sacrificed before going into the forest, and this, together with the use of certain charms that he carried in his hunting bundle, assured the desired result. While they were on the chase, the hunters smoked powdered roots as charms, various hunters preferring different charms. One of these, it was thought, lured a deer toward the hunter because the smoke from it resembled the smell of the deer's hoof. The hunters also used non-magical techniques. They blew moose and deer calls that imitated a fawn. This could be dangerous if a wolf or a wildcat came instead of the doe. Deer were also hunted at night, when they came to the stream or lake for water and to eat the pads and stems of water lilies. For this a jack light was used, the torch burning on a wooden platform in the front of a canoe with a darkened backstop behind it. The animal would pause, being momentarily dazed or attracted to the light. "Shining deer" was later outlawed by the U.S. Government except for Indians on Federal reservations.

In the "drive," a group of hunters would chop down trees to form a V; then they had their dogs run or drive the deer toward the apex of the V, where several hunters were waiting. A lone hunter sometimes set a snare with a slip noose in the deer trail. If there was snow on the ground the hunters carried the game home on small toboggans or, if light enough, trussed it up and carted it home on their backs by means of a tumpline.

Bears, when they were hunted, were shot, trapped in deadfalls, and occasionally captured in pitfalls. They were lured by such foods as honey, apples, pork, beaver musk, or other sweet-smelling or oily substance; a magic lure was also essential. Hunting bear was formerly considered a way in which a young man could prove his bravery, if he ventured into the cave in the spring and fought a hand-to-hand battle with the bear.

Winter was a busy time for the men as they kept check on their traps, removed the animals, changed the traps to new places, watched for fresh tracks, and studied the habits of the animals. They trapped small animals like the otter, beaver, mink, marten, and lynx, and birds like the partridge. Before steel traps came into use, deadfalls were arranged and

Flat bows. Chippewa.

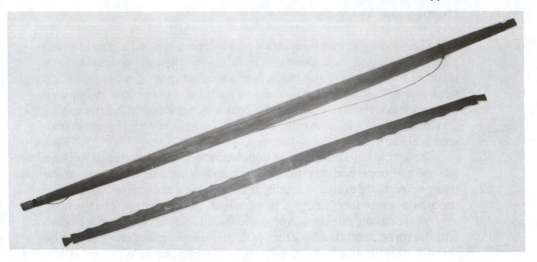

Moose call. Chippewa.

Deer call. Chippewa.

various nooses and nets contrived out of nettle-stalk-fiber and basswood-fiber twine.

When an Indian boy killed his first animal or bird, his parents held a Feast of the First Game. Prominent men of the tribe were invited to the Youth's Dance and, in this way, the boy was encouraged to be a good hunter and provider.

Much of the meat was boiled, in metal containers when they became available and, before that, in pottery vessels. Many of the Woodland Indians also took the stomach of an animal recently slain, filled it with water and pieces of meat, and then hung it over a slow fire. Birchbark kettles were used, too, hot stones being put into the water. Neither of these last-named types of container was very satisfactory, however, for they soon disintegrated. Spoons of wood, clam shells, and even birchbark were employed. If the food was too hot for the fingers, it was fished out of the stew with pointed sticks. Marrow, highly prized, was scooped out of the bones with a narrow willow stick. A tripod arrangement over the fire held the kettle, with a wooden hook and a heavy basswood-fiber cord being used in the old days.

Meat was roasted as well as boiled. It was also cut into thin slices, dried over a slow fire, and then pounded with a small stone on a larger, flat stone, and stored in birchbark containers. The tallow rendered from the fat was stored in the large intestine and bladder of the animal and then made into soap. Grease was used to season berries and wild rice. Even bones were pounded to a powder and mixed with dried meat and grease to be eaten later uncooked. The debris from each day's meals was scattered

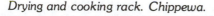

Drying and cooking rack. Chippewa.

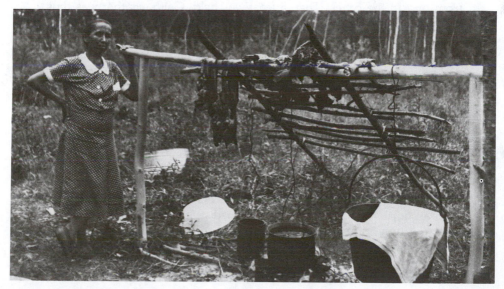

around to be cleaned up by the dogs. Nearly all the early explorers' journals mention the stench that arose from the Indian villages.

Most Indian groups ate but two meals a day. Later, when they had contact with the whites through logging camps, cranberry camps, and boarding schools, they grew accustomed to the idea of eating three times a day.

Wild Ricing

One of the food staples enjoyed particularly by the Chippewa and Menomini was wild rice, which is not a true rice but, rather, a cereal grass of the species *Zizania aquatica* growing in the shallow lakes and streams. It ripens in late summer, usually around the middle of August to early September.

Wild rice was so important to the Menomini that they became known as the Wild Rice people *(ma-nó-man,* wild rice). In their traditions this food was the gift of one of the Underneath beings, and sacrifices were necessary to insure a good harvest. When the rice was ready for harvesting, tobacco was offered to this spirit (it was put into a tiny hole dug for the purpose) and the chief asked for four days of good weather in which his people could gather the rice. After that, the Underneath spirits and the Thunderbirds could claim their share. The chief threw tobacco into the fire as an offering to the Thunderbirds, so they would not interfere with the weather. Skinner (1921, p. 144) says this was an unusual form of sacrifice, but with the Chippewa it was a common occurrence. After the speech, all the old people had a chance to smoke the tobacco as the pipe was passed from one to the other. Then a feast was held. Calm weather was thus assured, unless someone had not acted with due respect or had made excessive noises. Menstruating women were not allowed on the rice fields, nor were persons in whose families a death had occurred during the previous year.

In the morning the men set out in their canoes or, in later years, in double-ended rowboats, with a woman, to knock the rice. The woman sat in the prow of the canoe, facing the rear, while the man usually stood in the stern. Because it was impractical to try paddling through the dense rice stalks, he propelled the canoe with a crotched sapling from ten to sixteen feet long, and so he was able to grip the roots of the rice. With a twist of the pole he forced his boat through the tall stalks. The woman, using a cedar stick about three feet long, pulled bunches of rice over the gunwales and, with a shorter stick, knocked the ripened grain into the bottom of the canoe. It was hot and tiresome work, but they all moved with a rhythm they had learned as children. In the old days the men poled the canoes and the women and girls knocked the rice. In recent times, pairs of men sometimes worked together, as did pairs of women or young girls.

Each family had its particular rice field. Some of them traveled from one lake or stream to another, or gave permission to a relative to harvest rice in a certain place. Some groups appointed policemen to watch over the rice until it was ready for harvest; others merely had watchmen announce when it was ripe. When the chief was informed that the rice was ready to gather, he instructed the policemen to announce to the people: Tomorrow we will commence the harvest. All of these protective measures—the policemen, special feasts, and offerings—were necessary, for the Indians had to gather the rice before the waterfowl ate it or storms destroyed it. Each Indian, as he set out in the morning, automatically threw an additional pinch of tobacco into the water.

When the canoe was filled, the party returned to shore and, putting the rice into bark or wooden containers, they carried it back to their own section of the camp. Skinner says that formerly, on the first night, a small amount of rice was prepared and cooked, blessed by the chief, and then eaten by everyone assembled as a ritual offering to the spirits. Today, this feast of thanks apparently survives, as each family gives thanks when they eat the first of the new rice crop, but this is ordinarily after most of it has been prepared.

After the rice was cleaned of extraneous material—twigs, pieces of stalks, small stones, and worms, a hasty job and one at which everyone worked—it was spread out on sheets of birch bark, blankets or canvas to dry in the sun. When it was dry enough, the women put several pounds of rice in a big iron kettle or galvanized-iron washtub and parched it over an open fire. To keep it from scorching, they stirred it constantly with a wooden paddle. This parching process cured the rice and also helped loosen the outer husks. Final removal of the husks was accomplished by the man "dancing the rice." He donned specially made moccasins with high cuffs that were wrapped around the ankles. Then he stepped into a hole in the ground that had been lined with skin or, in more recent times, into a wooden lard tub sunk into the ground. Leaning on a diagonal post for support, he tramped on the rice, moving first on one foot and then the other. This "dancing" performance somewhat resembled a rumba motion. Formerly, this husking process was done with bare feet. One Chippewa informant slyly suggested that the Indians had become too soft from wearing shoes and, therefore, the ricing moccasins were devised.

The final chore was to separate the rice grains from their chaff, and this was done by the women on a breezy afternoon. Into large birchbark winnowing trays they placed a quantity of rice. With a flipping motion they moved the trays so that the rice kernels were tossed into the air, the chaff blew away, and the heavy grains sank to the bottom of the tray. Young girls just beginning to learn the process were roundly scolded if they allowed too much rice to fall to the ground.

For several weeks the family stayed in the ricing fields. There was a gay, almost a holiday, spirit, for, in spite of the hard work (gathering the rice in the morning, and parching, tramping, and winnowing it in the afternoon), there was always a multitude on the lake shore, with dancing and drumming at night, a chance to visit with families one had not seen for months.

Today most ricing fields are protected by the federal government and shared by all Indians equally, but many Indian families still return to the same fields that were allotted them by their tribal chiefs. Blackbirds and waterfowl, storms and periods of drought, all combine to determine a good or a bad rice harvest. Dams erected many miles away can also affect the harvest, for wild rice grows in the shallow parts of lakes and streams, maturing best if a fairly constant water level is maintained. At one time, among the Chippewa, it was a rather common practice to tie unripened sheaves of rice into a sort of "shepherd's crook." Densmore (1929, p. 128) wrote that this was done to establish the definite areas for each family, but one Chippewa informant said it also protected the grain from the birds and high water, and prevented the heavy winds from blowing the ripened rice into the lake. This meant extra work, however, and in most areas it is no longer done.

Wild rice was, and still is, a staple food for the Woodland Indians. They boiled it and ate it with corn, beans, or squash. Meat was often added, as was a small amount of grease and sometimes maple sugar for seasoning. As a treat, it was occasionally parched, like popcorn, and eaten without further cooking. The rice was stored in birchbark containers. At times, when a family wished to leave some in an area to which they knew they would return later in the year, they buried a dugout canoe full of rice on the sunny slope of a hill, so that rain water would drain off and not spoil the grain. It was said that rice cached in this way would keep as long as two years.

Father Marquette, in 1673, called the Menomini the "Nation of Wild Oats," and his description of their gathering and preparation of wild rice is very similar to the one given above.

3

The Life Cycle

Infancy

Jones (1917, p. 552) explains an obscure passage in a story told during the Medicine Dance, or mystic rite, by saying that a "child to be born of woman is preceded by its soul sent by the manitou; it enters its mother's womb. Without this, conception and birth are impossible . . ."

Among most Woodland tribes, a child was born in a special hut away from the main camp, for the blood connected with its birth was considered unclean, as was that of all females during their menstrual periods. A delivery rack stood ready—a smoothed pole two or three feet long set about two feet above ground on crotched posts. In her final labor the woman knelt on a reed mat padded with a blanket or hay, her chest against the crossbar. A few experienced women assisted her. After the umbilical cord was tied, a portion of it was saved so that later it could be sewn into a buckskin packet, generally diamond-shaped, which was hung on the hoop of the cradle board. The baby was bathed in a hot solution containing aromatic herbs and charred pieces of wood from a tree that had been hit by lightning.

The Potawatomi, as well as the other groups, observed pregnancy taboos. Both expectant parents, but particularly the mother, were enjoined not to look at deformed people or animals for fear the child might be born either with the deformity or dead. Eating or looking at turtles or rabbits could cause the baby to develop the jerky motion of a turtle or the fits of the rabbit. If a pregnant mother did happen to see an animal that was taboo, she saved a bit of the hair or flesh and later put in into hot water, in which she bathed the baby and thus nullified any harm that might have occurred. A pregnant Winnebago woman also was cautious about any exceptional activities. For instance, if she waded into a lake to search for water lily roots, she would protect the fetus by tying a lily root to her waist.

All through its infancy the child was kept close to its mother, and the daily relationship was extremely close. In order to protect it from death, the baby was given tiny moccasins with holes in the soles. Then, if death tried to lure the child away, it would be able to say: "But I can't come with you. See, my moccasins have holes in them!"

Almost immediately after birth, the baby was fastened to a cradle board, a cedar board about two feet long, ten inches wide, and three eights of an inch thick. A foot brace was fastened at one end, and a hickory hoop, which served to protect the head, was fastened near the other. Sphagnum moss, in a shallow birchbark tray, did double duty as both cushion and diaper; when necessary, the entire tray with its moss was discarded and a fresh one installed. The moss, commonly found in cranberry bogs, was dried to kill any insects, then pulled apart until it was soft and light. In winter the baby's feet were wrapped in rabbit skin with the hair inside, or in soft cattail down. The infant was placed on the padding and securely bound with two wrappers, either of buckskin or cloth, each wrapper being slipped through a thong attached to the edge of the board, then wound around both the board and the baby and tied with buckskin strips or woven yarn strips about an inch wide. The wrappers were decorated by the mother in floral designs of quill or beadwork. The baby was completely bound, with only its head showing, but later its arms were freed. This, said the Indians, kept it out of trouble, kept it warm, and tended to hold the back, arms, and legs straight—important physical characteristics.

The cradle board served as a bed as well as a baby carriage. When the mother went on a journey, she slung it on her back and held it in position by means of a buckskin tumpline. When she worked around the wigwam or the camp, she placed the cradle board against a tree. Should the board accidentally fall over, the hoop protected the baby's head. The child could watch its mother at work and, in addition, gaze at the little playthings hanging on the hoop. There were usually three kinds: those intended solely for amusement (little shells or birchbark cones), gifts given by the person who had named the baby and who had a definite reason for his gift, and the "charms," foremost of which was the little pouch containing the umbilical cord. There were many reasons for retaining this cord. A child gained wisdom by keeping the cord near him or on his person. It was thought that if he did not guard it, he would always be searching for something, and some said he would "become foolish" without it. If a baby died, the mother often kept the pouch containing its umbilical cord, and treasured it for years. Some of these pouches were decorated with a butterfly design, the symbol of childish play.

At short intervals during the day the baby was taken off the cradle board for cleaning and exercise, but more than one informant said that their babies cried to be put back onto the board. The baby was even nursed while on the board. Although the time varied with each tribe, on the whole the child was kept on the board until it was from nine months to a year or more. When ropes and blankets became common, a small hammock was fashioned by slinging a blanket between ropes and putting a wooden crosspiece at either end. These were used outdoors as well as in the lodge.

Child wrapped on a cradle board. Chippewa.

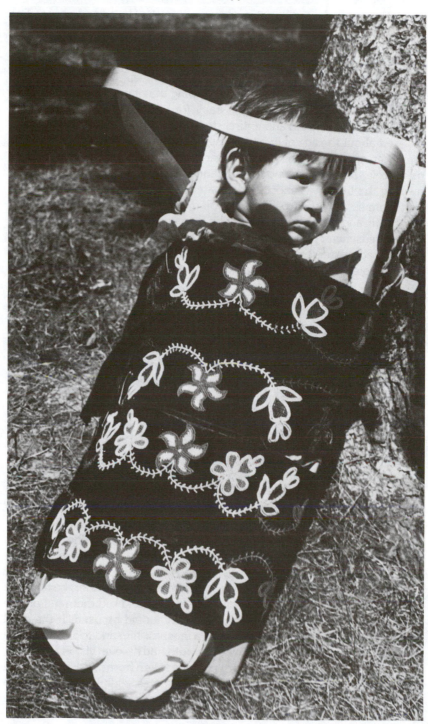

The cradle board has disappeared from the Woodland scene. The last record we have of its use among the Wisconsin Chippewa is 1939. In 1940 Robert Ritzenthaler purchased a cradle board for the Milwaukee Public Museum, but he had trouble with his movie camera and could get no pictures of it being used. He returned the next year to the same woman and took the cradle board with him, knowing that it was one of the last on the reservation. By this time, the baby for whom it was designed was two-and-a-half years old and entirely too large for it, but he got his picture.

At about the age of two the baby was weaned, although occasionally a mother nursed her child for a longer period. As contact with the white man grew, and with the advent of canned milk, the length of time spent nursing the baby was shortened; in later times the children were nursed only from six months to a year or a bit more. The baby was weaned on a fish broth and wild rice boiled until it was very soft.

Grease was rubbed on a baby thought to be ailing, goose oil being considered particularly effective. To guard against chaffing, the finely ground powder from rotten oak was dusted on.

Naming

A child received a name or names in several ways, and, as dreams were extremely important to the Woodland Indians, they played an integral part in the naming. Generally the parents called in a paid namer, one whose dreams had given him power. A small group of friends and relatives offered tobacco and food to the spirits, then ate. Then the namer took the child on his lap and named him. The name would carry no special power for the child, but it was meant to benefit him since it placed him under the protection of the namer's guardian spirit. Occasionally the name was even omitted inadvertently during the ceremony, for the important thing was that the child receive some advantage from the dream. A special relationship existed between the child and his namer: each called the other "my namesake," *nia we'ɛ* in Chippewa. The namer would give a boy, for instance, a little drum or a tiny set of bow and arrows. These articles, which were among those hung on the cradle board, were referred to by an express term in Chippewa, *ishiu'winǝn,* and they were kept throughout the owner's life, to be honored at feasts. When the boy grew older, he took the sacred objects to a War Dance or special feasts and laid them out on the floor with food. This was the only time they would be used. If the child became ill at any time, the namer gave a feast for him and took advantage of his own curing power. Later, when a youth had his own vision as a result of his puberty fast, he acquired a name, one taken from incidents that had occurred in his dream. This name, however, was seldom used, although the owner could, in turn, bestow it or a similar one on children when he grew to manhood.

Parents often gave their child a "namesake name," perhaps one they had dreamed, but it was not done ceremonially, and the name possessed no power. It was closely associated with a nickname, or common name, the name by which most Indians were known throughout their lives. These were often based on incidents that took place in early years, perhaps the name of an animal (marten or lynx) or of a person who came into the baby's wigwam shortly after birth. Sometimes the child was given the name of a certain bird whose movements seemed to be similar to those of the baby. These names often carried an element of humor or suggested obvious physical characteristics.

In the old days, some chiefs were known by the name of their gens, or kinship group. Chief Oshkosh, the famous Menomini chief, was named for his moiety, the use of which term is described in chapter 4.

As they came into closer contact with the whites, many Indians took English and French names, sometimes mispronouncing them so they had a flavor all their own. Margaret became Magid and Sophia became Sope. The whites, too, were responsible for the literal translations into English of Indian names like Hole-in-the-Sky, Little Bear, Crotched Tree. Surnames, in many instances, were acquired as the result of the need for a name on the payroll records in the lumber camps. In a number of cases the Indians took first names of whites as surnames. Indian Jim's children became known as Charley and Pete Jim, while others bore the surnames of Frank, George, Mike, and Andy. Other surnames were devised from such Indian names as Manomen, Nahbahkah, Weewasin and Kesick (Geezhik); and some simply took over undistinctive white names like Johnson, Smith, and Williams. Many an Indian woman acquired her surname through marriage with a white man.

Childhood

All through childhood the Indian boys and girls learned from their parents, their doting grandparents, their brothers, and, more often, sisters, as well as respected older members of the tribe. Children were treated well and frequently indulged. A permissive upbringing is characteristic of the American Indian in general. The parents seldom raised their voices to reprimand a child, and corporal punishment was equally rare. What would be treated as a catastrophic event by a white parent was regarded with casual calmness by the Indian. An observed example was that of a Potawatomi child who tripped and fell, receiving a rather nasty gash. The crying child ran into the house, where the father said, in a soft voice, "Why didn't you look where you were going?" He then treated the wound. The mother made no comment, but went on with her work. This lack of tension on the part of Indian parents was reflected in the personality pattern of the child during his youth and later as an adult; it seems to account for what is popularly and tritely, but not wholly inaccurately, called the "stoic" in the Indian.

On the whole, boys were taught by their fathers how to fish and trap, and their roles as hunters were conditioned from infancy. The Kickapoo, as well as other tribes, tied a miniature bow and arrow on the hoop of a boy's cradle board, and, shortly after he learned to walk, they gave him a small but operational bow. Both boys and girls were warned not to disturb birds' nests or the young of animals, for these, too, had a place in the scheme of things. At an early age they learned how to recognize the plants, how to gather and dry them, and which ones had medicinal value. They were expected to fast while still quite young, so that, when it was time for the vision quest, they would be receptive. They were encouraged to dream and to relate their dreams, so they would know what to look for and to recognize a vision when it appeared. Fasting also prepared the children for the difficult times when there was little food to be had. When the men were on a hunt, they asked their children at home to fast on their behalf, for this assured good luck. Children were admonished not to gaze longingly at the food that other people were eating. Repeatedly they were told to be cheerful, to keep busy at useful occupations, to respect their elders, to be gentle and quiet so as not to disturb others in the crowded wigwam at night; nor were they to peek into other wigwams. It was imperative, also, in times of impending danger or when exposed to sudden fright, that children be able to remain perfectly still.

Some tribes had a sort of "town crier," who went through the camp after dark telling the young men who were courting that it was time to go home. He recited moral precepts to be observed by the young people and announced what would take place the next day. If he knew that some of the youths had misbehaved, he spoke of the mischief without mentioning names and suggested that they mend their ways. He warned against stealing and against the use of firewater, and advised them to be moderate in smoking tobacco, to be respectful to women, and to obey their parents. Women were cautioned not to quarrel with each other.

Fright was exploited as a common device to train children. At night, for instance, small children were told the owl would carry them away if they did not go right to sleep or if they did not behave themselves. An owl mask effectively intimidated young children, and most Chippewa children still fear the owl. A man called the frightener was dressed in ragged clothes, used a cane, and wore either an ugly mask with a big nose or a birchbark mask that, on late summer evenings, looked very pale. With this he scared the children into leaving their play and returning to their wigwams. Ugly or frightening forms were placed near areas considered too dangerous for the children to play in, and these were effective in keeping the youngsters nearer home.

While fathers taught their sons how to live, mothers were equally solicitous in raising their daughters. Girls learned how to make a wigwam, how to chop wood and carry it back to camp, how to gather berries and roots, how to make birchbark vessels, and how to prepare buckskin, sew it into clothing, and decorate it. They were also instructed in all the other tasks in the woman's domain. If a girl was able to do these things, she generally made a good marriage, for her reputation would be spread abroad, and the young men would seek her out.

Dolls were not only playthings, but were essential in helping an Indian girl learn the customs of her tribe. She made buckskin dresses for them, leggings and moccasins, beaded and porcupine quill decorations. The dolls themselves were made from a variety of materials. Some were of bark, from the slippery elm or the birch, while others were of green basswood leaves in the summer and of bright autumn leaves in the fall.

Woman scraping a buckskin. Chippewa.

Making a makuk. Menomini.

Roots of the bulrush were partially dried and then tied with basswood fiber to resemble a human figure. Bunches of grass as well as tufts of pine needles (usually the Norway pine) were tied in such a way that they made a very respectable-looking doll. Even willow withes were utilized for this purpose. Buckskin and, later, cloth were fashioned into dolls and then stuffed with soft moss.

There were other playthings, too, most of which are described in the section on "Games." The small bows and arrows the boys received while still quite young were indispensable in training them for later hunts as well as for war.

When a boy killed his first game, his parents gave a Feast of the First Game. A few of the prominent old men were invited to an unpretentious meal, perhaps a bit of rice and some blueberries together with the rabbit or bird the boy had killed. The old men then talked to the *manidog*, the spirits, and asked that the boy and his family be granted certain favors.

About the time of puberty a boy was encouraged to go into the forest for several days at a time, fast during the day, and dream at night. At "breakfast" he was offered either food or charcoal; if he chose to fast, he took the charcoal and rubbed it on his cheeks to indicate that he was on a vision quest. To stay out for four days in a row was highly desirable. On the first day a father often went to help his son prepare a small shelter or a nest in a tree. Many fathers went back periodically to be sure their sons were all right. By this time the boy had already experienced some sort of dream and knew what to expect. There were few examples of failure, although a youth might be forced to try several times before he had a real vision. The fast was either a complete one or one with very little water and almost no food, except after sundown, and then only a small amount. Most informants said that "this cleared the mind" after several days, so they were able to see the vision, or hear the name, or hear a song and remember it.

The fasting dream, or vision quest, was of the utmost significance to the individual. The dream gave him a guardian spirit who would guide and protect him the rest of his life; it equipped him, in some cases, with the power to cure or to harm (if necessary); it granted him the ability to prophesy, and it provided him with a supply of songs and names. The guardian spirit would be painted on his personal drum. Among the Winnebago, one acquired only the guardian spirit from his first fast and perhaps, in addition, a name. Other favors were gained through the years by additional fasting. The favors received through fasting involved obligations as well on the part of the recipient. He was expected to honor his guardian spirit with frequent offerings of food and, particularly, tobacco. Maintaining good rapport with his own guardian spirit and with other spirits was always uppermost in the mind of the religious Indian, and he manifested this by his daily actions.

When the girl was ready for her first menses, she went for four days and nights (among the Potawatomi she stayed as long as ten days) to a little wigwam her mother had built away from the main camp. She probably would have had some fasting experience before this time (although not specifically for a vision, as did the boys), but if she had a vision, it was considered a special blessing. Ordinarily a girl asked the *manidog* to reward her with a long life, a good husband, and a large number of healthy children. In her puberty hut she was allowed almost no food, taking only a little water. More recently, a female relative would take a bit of food to the menstrual hut after dark. The girl was not supposed to scratch herself with her hands, but to use a stick provided for the purpose. Radin (1916, p. 137) quotes a Winnebago informant, a male, who said that a girl's lover would visit her in the menstrual lodge, an unusual situation indeed, since the menstruating woman was regarded as a contaminating influence among other groups, and, even today, the practice of having such a woman eat her meals away from others is still observed to some extent. Eating a meal with a menstruating woman or drinking from a cup she had used could cause sickness, especially paralysis.

When the girl returned to her parents' lodge, a feast was held. In some groups she was not allowed to taste any fruit or berries gathered during the summer until she had gone through the proper ceremony. A small amount of fruit was placed before each person, the *Mide'* priest and other guests, but the girl could not touch hers. The *Mide'* priest, after drumming and singing, put some to her mouth, but withdrew it as she started to take it. Four times he did this before allowing her any fruit the fifth time. Patience and self discipline were the tenets being underscored here. All through the first summer following a girl's reaching maturity, this ritual was followed with the first of all natural products, including wild rice.

Courtship and Marriage

Ordinarily marriages were arranged by the family of the young man. Although marriage within the clan was banned, cross-cousin marriage, or marriage between the children of a brother and his sister, was practiced by nearly all the Woodland groups in the early days (Callender, 1962, p. 60). The coming of the Europeans had some effect upon the demise of this practice, but cross-cousin relationships remained strong, as was evidenced by kinship terms, joking relationships, and giftgiving between cross-uncles and their nieces. Most marriages were monogamous, but polygyny was sanctioned, and an important man could have two or, rarely, three wives. The sororate, the custom of a man marrying a sister of his deceased wife, was also practiced.

Apparently Woodland Indian girls were quite modest in their relations with young men, for they were closely watched by their mothers and grandmothers. When a young man began to show interest in a girl, he spoke first to the other people living next door. From them he must have gained a fairly accurate assessment of the girl's abilities and whether or not she possessed the qualities he was seeking in a wife. When he called on the girl in the evening, he always talked to her in the middle of her lodge, with all the adults nearby. If the call was a late one, the mother or grandmother would stir up the fire and sit nearby, smoking her pipe. The young people were always conscious of being watched. "Courting flutes" were popular, but the girl could not leave her lodge when she heard one being played. Its sound carried so well that the young men were able to withdraw to the edge of the village to serenade the girls of their choice.

As the youth grew serious in his pursuit of the girl, he brought her parents a deer or some other animal he had killed, an indication of his ability to provide for a family. If he was asked to stay and partake of the meal, he was assured of the parents' approval and could come and go more freely than before. The Potawatomi youth brought the girl a blanket, and, if she allowed him to put it over her shoulders, it meant that she agreed to marry him. Although it is said that formerly love matches were rare, there seems to have been a good deal of courting at night. Gifts were often exchanged between the couple's parents—clothing and finery for the women, a horse and, in later times, possibly, a buggy for the bride's parents.

Marriage involved no formal ceremony, the couple merely going off by themselves for a few days. Perhaps they went to a lodge of their own, but on the whole they lived, for a while at least, with the girl's parents. Occasionally a young married couple lived with the husband's parents. During the early part of the twentieth century the Indian Bureau began recognizing common-law marriage. If a man and a woman lived together as man and wife, but without marriage rites, the union was recognized as legal by the Bureau and was recorded as "marriage by Indian custom."

Separations were easy, for if a couple could not agree, the woman merely returned to her father's lodge. Skinner (1921, p. 55) reports that a wife could be given away publicly with a blanket at the Drum Dance. In recent times, with the continuing breakdown of the old customs, marriages were somewhat brittle, and many people were married two or three times. Bachelorhood or spinsterhood was infrequent—in fact, almost unheard of.

The "joking relationship" was carried on between brothers- and sisters-in-law, uncles and aunts, nieces and nephews, and cross-cousins. Brothers- and sisters-in-law, especially, were expected to exchange jokes, some with slightly sexual overtones. According to Radin, the mother-in-law taboo was practiced in limited form among the Winnebago, but it is not reported elsewhere.

Old Age

Some old people lived by themselves, some with their married offspring. There seems to have been no general pattern. It was an advantage to a younger couple to have the grandparents with them, for the woman could help with the children, the clothing, and other craft work and with the lighter household tasks, while the man could teach the younger boys. In more recent years the old age pension check was sometimes the only constant source of revenue for an entire family.

Death, Burial, and Mourning

When someone died, his hair was braided, and his body was washed and dressed in his best clothing and wrapped in sheets of birch bark or, later, cloth. Beadwork of every kind was placed on him and his *Mide'* bag (if he belonged to that society) tucked under his arm. Sometimes the Chippewa painted the face, moccasins, and blanket with a brown fungus and vermillion. A round spot of brown went on each cheek with a red line drawn through it horizontally. This custom (Densmore, 1929, p. 74) apparently started after a woman recovered from a trance during which, she said, she had visited the land of the northern lights. These emanations were really dancing ghosts, the women gaily dressed and the warriors holding their war clubs. The ghostly faces were painted with brown fungus.

A section of the wigwam wall—always toward the west, since the land of the dead was located there—was removed so that the body could be taken out to the grave. Articles that he had especially valued during his lifetime were placed with the corpse, perhaps his gun and certainly his tobacco pouch, flint and steel, or matches. Even small children had tobacco pressed into each tiny fist. A woman might have a favorite ax, needles, or a pack strap buried with her. In all cases a few essentials such as a kettle, dish, and spoon needed for a four-day journey would be arranged next to the body.

The kind of funeral ceremony depended on the society to which the deceased had belonged. The Peyote society, the Drum Dance, the *Mide'* society, each had its special ritual, but there were some elements observed that were common to them all. Certain songs and speeches were delivered by the priests and addressed directly to the spirit of the deceased, since the spirit stayed near its body for some time. Although it would take four days for the soul to traverse the "road of souls," interment was done as soon as possible after death.

After the deceased had been warned of the dangers on the four-day journey, the body was carried away from the main camp to the spot where a grave about four feet deep had been prepared. It was interred, and

Wooden house erected over grave. Chippewa.

covered with dirt and more bark, which was pinned down with heavy stones to protect the body from animals. Even logs were sometimes used as a protective cover. In historic times a little wooden house about five feet long and two or three feet high was erected over the grave. The grave itself was always oriented along the east-west axis. A small opening was cut in the west end for egress of the soul. Under this hole was a shelf for holding food—maple syrup, wild rice, and fruits—and tobacco, which would be needed by the soul during its four-day journey. People who did not have much to eat, and children, were allowed to help themselves to this food. Sometimes a dead person's relatives would suggest to their friends that they visit a certain grave for some food.

The *Mide'* priest carved a grave marker that pictured the totem of the deceased—an animal, bird, or fish carved or drawn upside down to denote death. On some graves a "brave-stick" was placed. This was a stick about three feet long; four areas were whittled so that the shavings projected upward, and between the whittled areas were four red stripes representing blood. The brave-stick was a sign to dead warriors already in heaven to protect and help the soul on its journey. These were the warrior foes who had been slain by the deceased's friends and relatives. Exploits—four were necessary—were recounted by the men who had done the slaying. These dead warriors not only protected the dead soul, but also acted as servants, building fires at night and preparing the food.

When the Indians began living in houses instead of wigwams, the corpse was laid in a simple coffin paid for by the government, but the body was not embalmed, because the funds did not cover this. The coffin was carried out a west window. It was never taken out the door for fear that the dead soul, still hovering nearby, would snatch someone else to carry away in death.

On the first day of the four-day journey, the soul would be confronted by a quaking log laid across a stream; some groups said this would occur on the last day, and some said the log was really a snake, the dreaded Water Monster. If the soul addressed the log as "grandfather" and threw tobacco into the water, the log would stop trembling and the soul could cross in safety and meet his escort to heaven. This was *Chibia'bos* (in Potawatomi), the younger brother of the Woodland culture hero, *Wi'ske* (in Potawatomi, and called *Wenebojo* by the Chippewa, *Manabush* by the Menomini, and other names by other groups). *Chibia-'bos* lives in the West, while *Wi'ske* resided in the East. Each evening the soul would have to stop, prepare a fire with matches provided by his relatives, and eat some of the food. If he had the dead warriors to help him, so much the better. At the grave, meanwhile, each evening around sundown a fire was built symbolizing the fact that the bereaved ones were joining the soul in a meal. The actual feast, however, was not held until the fourth evening. At the end of the fourth day, the soul entered heaven, a large village of Indians where he joined the souls of his relatives and friends. His guide, *Chibia'bos,* informed the soul that he could stay here forever, where there was no trouble or sickness, where everyone was happy, and where, as Skinner says, he could play lacrosse forever.

The first mourning was often accompanied by much wailing and even laceration of the flesh with flint knives. Regular mourning was observed for about a year and then terminated by a ceremony. Men could not handle medicines or weapons while they were in mourning. They often painted their entire faces black, but, if only in partial mourning, they merely painted a black circle around each eye. A widowed woman also painted her face black and was not to marry until after the charcoal had worn off. Pine resin was usually added to the ashes, making them last longer. Sometimes the hair above the forehead was cropped short; women usually let their hair hang loose during the mourning period. They wore old clothes and refrained from going to public places. No one in mourning could go to the wild rice fields for fear of offending the spirits. One in mourning was not allowed to touch a child after the removal ceremony, for this could cause the child's illness or even death. Most Indians had a great love for children, so if this taboo was ever broken, it undoubtedly would have been accidental.

The ceremony for "restoring the mourners" was held once a year, and all those who had lost relatives were publicly comforted, presented with bright shawls and ornaments, and then fed ceremoniously. After that they could eat as usual and mingle with everyone.

Keeping a "spirit bundle" was another way of showing respect for the dead, but not everyone observed this custom. A lock of hair was cut from the back of the deceased's head soon after death and, wrapped in birchbark, it became the nucleus of the spirit bundle. Relatives built a special fire on the first night and talked to the spirit bundle. For four consecutive nights this was done. The mother of a dead child sometimes

Fresh grave. Potawatomi.

made a spirit bundle, carried it around with her, and placed food before it. A widow would treat her husband's spirit bundle as though his spirit were in it, placing food before it and laying it next to her body at night. She added to the bundle through the year by wrapping around it new beadwork, cloth, blankets, or anything of value. At the end of the year, she took this bundle to her husband's people and asked them to release her from mourning. If they felt she had been flighty or insincere in her mourning, they could require her to carry the bundle still longer. If they agreed to release her, a feast was given and all the articles in the bundle were distributed among her husband's relatives. They, in turn, washed her, gave her new clothing, painted her face, and declared that she was free to marry again if she chose. The levirate, or marriage of a widow to her husband's brother, was the preferred custom. The lock of hair that had formed the bundle's nucleus was buried, still in its birchbark wrapping, next to the grave of the deceased.

Men sometimes carried a spirit bundle, but a much smaller one. A man with two wives seldom carried a spirit bundle, but the wife's mother would carry it for her daughter, the goods being supplied by the husband.

4

Social Organization

The Woodland settlement pattern was one of rather small, semisedentary groups living together. In the literature such settlements are referred to sometimes as "villages," sometimes as "bands"; their true nature is not always clear. In the instance of a recognized community or series of communities under definite political leadership, the term "band" seems most appropriate. The majority of the Woodland tribes were small, seldom containing over a few thousand people, and rarely did they assemble in large groups. There were exceptions: during the summertime, when several hundred people might live together, and during a time of major warfare. For religious events, especially Medicine Dance, a large group might assemble. A lacrosse game also attracted a large group, but living and activities were essentially small-group operations. The larger tribes, such as the Chippewa, were divided into many small bands having little communication with other bands and no over-all tribal organization or leadership. The term "atomistic" has been applied to the Woodland way of life, and, while it has stirred some controversy, it has a certain general validity. The Prairie tribes differed somewhat in having less seasonal movement, and, at least in the historic period, they placed more emphasis on established village life. Another reason for them to assemble was their spring buffalo hunt.

Woodland society was kin oriented, with patterns of interpersonal relations almost exclusively those of kinship. Ties of blood and marriage bound the group into a network of relationships, each with its appropriate behavior pattern. Ordinarily, everyone in the local community was related. Kinship ties also formed bonds between the various communities. With certain exceptions, the Chippewa for example, and with some variations, the Woodland kinship system can be categorized as of the Omaha type, with terminology classificatory and nongenerational. Separate terms distinguished children of a brother from those of a sister. Cross-cousin marriage was preferred; thus, the children of a brother were prospective mates for the children of his sister, but marriage was prohibited between parallel cousins: the children of a brother's brother or those of a sister's sister.

Kinship involved certain behavioral patterns. Respect was a requisite between siblings of opposite sex, children and parents, and between children-in-law and their parents-in-law. Thus a feeling of mutual respect and deference was expected between brother and sister, and this was intensified after puberty. Brothers and sisters also played an important role in initiating or conferring approval on each other's marriages. Joking relationships existed. A brother-in-law, for instance, was expected to joke with his sister-in-law, and often the jokes were quite ribald. Teasing, accompanied by gift exchanges, was a form of behavior between a niece or nephew and the cross-aunt or cross-uncle. The aunt or uncle was preferred as counsel for any problems the niece or nephew might encounter. The first time a boy went out on a war party, he nearly always chose to follow his maternal uncle. The same warm, intimate relationship also existed between grandparents and their grandchildren.

In addition to marriage, ceremonial adoption provided another mechanism for extending kinship. A friend, but never a relative, of a deceased person was adopted by the family and granted certain kinship rights and obligations, although he retained his own as well as keeping his own name and residence. A replacement technique such as this is based on the assumption that a kinship society functions most efficiently when all positions are filled.

This was also a classless, egalitarian society, although certain individuals, like chiefs, priests, and shamans, were accorded more respect on the basis of their positions, knowledge, abilities, or greater rapport with the supernatural forces. There was no institution of slavery, as was found among tribes of the Northwest Coast, where captives from another tribe occupied lowly positions as slaves.

The smallest social unit was the nuclear family: husband, wife or wives, and their unmarried children. Among some groups a year of bride service was involved, during which time the couple lived with the wife's parents, serving as contributors to the household. They then set up an independent dwelling nearby, ordinarily creating a residence pattern of matrilocally extended families living in adjacent households. What might be termed a microcommunity was thus composed of a number of families related by blood or marriage, co-operating particularly in hunting and food gathering. A number of adjacent microcommunities, under a political leader, made up a band.

In addition to his family affiliations, every individual was a member of a clan: a unilineal group with stipulated descent. These were patrilineal and exogamous. Thus, a man of the Wolf clan was required to marry a woman from a different clan, but their children would belong to the Wolf clan. Among the Prairie tribes, the clan was a ceremonial unit and had a naming function. Each clan had a stock of personal names from which the parents could choose, so long as it was not used by anyone else. Upon the individual's death, his name reverted to the clan pool. Each clan had one or more sacred bundles containing items with supernatural power that could be drawn upon for mutual help; these were refurbished ceremonially at regular intervals. The functions of the clan among the Forest tribes is less well known. They served mainly to regulate marriage; the functions of providing names and operating as ceremonial units, as in the Prairie groups, were only weakly developed. However, the function of providing names was found among the Winnebago and, in very attenuated form, among the Menomini. Among the Winnebago, certain clans also had prescribed duties and responsibilities: the Thunderbird clan functioned to preserve peace, the Bear clan was in charge of disciplinary action and policing, and the Warrior clan was in charge of war activities. The Winnebago also held clan feasts, at which offerings were made to the clan animal. The Forest tribes had sacred bundles but, in contrast to the Prairie groups, they were not associated with clans.

Clans were grouped into exogamous phratries. The nineteen clans of the Menomini, for example, were organized into seven phratries, one phratry, for instance, consisting of the Great Ancestral Bear, Snapping Turtle, and Porcupine clans. The Great Ancestral Bear clan was the leader of this particular phratry and gave it its name. Members of the same phratry had obligations of providing one another with hospitality and mutual assistance.

Dual Division

The majority of the Woodland tribes were divided into dual divisions called moieties, which took two distinct forms. The Winnebago, Menomini, and Miami were divided into Earth and Sky moieties on the basis of clan. Thus, the clans named for those creatures that dwelt in the sky formed one division, and those named after land dwellers, water-inhabiting animals, or fish formed the second division. According to Radin (1923, p. 187) there were only two functions of the Winnebago dual system: that of marriage regulation—that is, one had to marry into the opposite moiety—and, possibly, that of reciprocal burial. Radin also found evidence that at one time the Winnebago moieties lived in separate halves of the village.

The moieties of the Prairie tribes were not based on clan but were assigned by order of birth. Among the Fox, for example, if the father belonged to the White moiety, the first-born child was assigned to the Black, the next-born to the White, and so on. The moieties functioned in game rivalries, particularly in lacrosse, with the Whites competing against the Blacks. The moiety system, in addition, also provided an alignment for rivalry in war honors.

There is no record of moieties for the Chippewa, the Ottawa, or the Forest Potawatomi.

Government

Chieftainship followed hereditary lines. The Winnebago selected their chiefs from certain families within the Thunderbird clan, the Menomini from the principal family of the Great Mythical Bear clan. Among the Chippewa and Potawatomi a son of a deceased chief replaced his father. Information is scanty regarding the selection process. It appears most probable that the chief was selected by the council from a number of hereditary candidates on the basis of personal qualities and abilities.

The duties of the chief were purely civil, although he had the power to intercede in the event that a war leader wanted to engage in a war that the chief felt was unnecessary. His major role was one of maintaining peace and order in the community, making decisions, and determining a course of action with regard to the welfare of the tribe. During the treaty-making period with the whites, he was the tribal representative, as well as the one who signed the treaties. In any significant decisions the chief was aided by the clan, band, or tribal council.

In general, political organization was not highly developed among the Woodland Indians, and chieftainship was of a relatively weak nature. There was little need for strong civil leadership, and it was not unusual for a shaman or priest to exert greater influence and possess greater prestige than the chief. Among the Woodland chiefs of historical importance, their primary role as chief seemed to be that of providing leadership in the wars against the white man. Black Hawk, a subordinate chief of the Sauk and Fox, led his people in the Black Hawk war of 1832; Tecumseh, the son of a Shawnee chief, organized a series of tribes in the Indiana Territory against the American forces in the early nineteenth century; Pontiac, an Ottawa leader during the mid-eighteenth century, organized a number of tribes against the British forts, including the famous six-month siege at Fort Detroit in 1763.

War

In the days of intertribal warfare, the war leaders were men who felt called upon to lead a war party as the result of a dream or vision. Their leadership was temporary, lasting only for the duration of the raid, and they relied upon charismatic qualities of personality and reputation in assembling their party. Warriors of established reputation were pressed into police duty, either within the camp or to prevent the premature harvesting of wild rice. Among such tribes as the Menomini, the war power was vested in the owners of war bundles (Skinner, 1921, p. 51).

War itself consisted of sorties made by relatively small raiding parties operating on a hit-and-run basis, and it was engaged in for two reasons: to avenge a slain member of the tribe or to gain personal war honors. There was little loss of life. An individual organized his war party by sending to the nearby villages a messenger who explained the purpose of the mission to the assembled warriors. Those who wished to join the party took the proffered pipe and tobacco from the messenger and smoked it. Then, at an appointed time, the volunteers met at the leader's lodge for a feast, where they were given a fuller explanation of the mission and a chance to offer their final pledge.

The Menomini conducted pre-raid ceremonies in which the party assembled at a certain spot in the forest. There they erected a lodge of boughs, displayed the open war bundle, sacrificed and ate a dog, performed the war dance, and related their former deeds of valor. The party then moved out. When they neared the enemy camp, which had been sought out by advance scouts, they reopened the war bundle and, after singing the special songs associated with the bundle, they distributed its contents to the warriors. One man might receive a snakeskin to give him stealth, another a root to chew on to make him invulnerable. There were many such items that aided the warriors in a magical way.

Just before dawn the attack would begin. The warriors would rush the enemy camp with clubs and bows and arrows, unprotected by such devices as shields or armor. Those who killed a foe were accorded the highest honor—an eagle feather to be worn in the hair. The Menomini awarded a wampum belt to the man who killed the first enemy. The Winnebago granted war honors for counting "coup," or striking a fallen enemy, a custom popular among the Indians of the Plains. The Iroquois practice of taking captives for adoption or torture was not customary among the Algonkian-speaking tribes.

Scalping was common. A circular portion of the scalp was cut from the crown of the enemy's head. On the homeward journey it was stretched on a hoop, and, back at the village, all the scalps were carried on sticks or poles in a Scalp Dance. After this, the warriors gave them to a female relative. Occasionally they were added to the war bundle. The Chippewa and Winnebago had the custom of planting the scalp poles at the grave of a slain warrior, where they were left to disintegrate.

Although warfare never attained the prominence it did among the Plains tribes, it was still accorded considerable importance in the Woodland value system. A successful warrior was assured of respect and prestige in his tribes, and, for the rest of his life, at certain public ceremonies it was his privilege to relate his heroic feats.

Wooden effigy bowl. Winnebago.

Woodland moccasins.

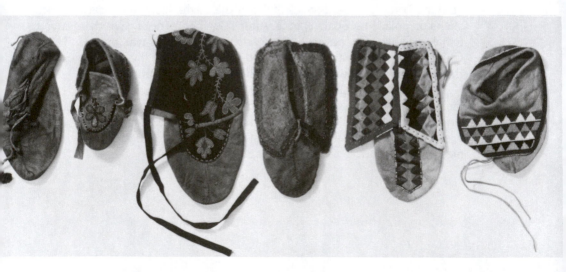

5

Material Culture

Woodland material culture was relatively simple, and it is often forgotten that a staggering amount of time and effort was spent in merely gathering all the materials needed for clothing, shelter, tools, items of transport, and other essentials for living. Then, when these had been collected, more hours were devoted to the manufacture of the various articles.

Although they were concerned more with utility than aesthetics, the Woodland groups exhibited considerable skill and some flair for the decorative arts, as shown in the women's weaving, leatherwork, quillwork, beadwork, and ribbonwork. Pottery, judging from precontact remains, was crude in technique, form, and decoration. The men produced an array of serviceable wooden artifacts ranging from simple bowls to the complicated birchbark canoe. Their artistic endeavors were confined largely to sculpturing human and animal figures on bowls and ladles, and the freestanding fetish figurines. In painting their drumheads, the men were more concerned with religious purposes than a display of technique or beauty. In historic times, they showed some artistry in fashioning ornaments out of German silver. Contrasted to those of the Southwest, however, Woodland arts and crafts have attracted little attention or interest on the part of the outside world. This may be due, perhaps, to the limited amount of painting and sculpture deemed worthy of the art gallery. Neither were their products particularly adaptable, ornamentally, for the white man's personal wear, as was Navaho silverwork, or for household use, as were Navaho rugs and Hopi pottery.

Men's Clothing

The basic attire for the men included a breechclout, leggings, and moccasins, all of tanned buckskin. The breechclout was a strip of buckskin, about eighteen inches by four feet, which was passed between the legs and up and over a thong or belt, leaving a sort of apron to flap free in the front and back. This flap was often decorated with quillwork. During postcontact times, cloth was increasingly substituted for buckskin, and, beginning with the early twentieth century, a square panel or apron worn front and back became a popular replacement for the breechclout. With the switch to cloth, beads and ribbonwork were used more and more as decoration.

Leggings were made by folding a rectangular piece of buckskin lengthwise down the center. The open edges were sewn together, with a margin narrow at the hip end but gradually widening as it reached the ankle. The residual edges formed flaps, about two inches wide at the top to around six inches at the bottom, and these were cut into fringes. The leggings were often decorated with beaded embroidery or ribbon applique', and they were fastened to the belt with buckskin thongs. On dress occasions, loom-beaded bands or garters were fastened around the leggings below the knees. Sometimes cloth was substituted for buckskin, but both survived into modern times.

In contrast to the stiff, rawhide sole of the Plains moccasin, the sole of the Woodland moccasin was soft, both sole and sides consisting of a single piece of buckskin with a seam up the back, while the upper front was completed in one of two styles. In one basic style, an elliptical piece, serving as a vamp, was added, and another piece was sewn to the back half to serve as a cuff. Only the vamps and cuffs were decorated with quillwork or beadwork. For the Forest tribes there were two variations of this style, determined by the size of the vamp and the method of attaching it. In one variation a long, wide vamp was sewn on, in puckered fashion, to cover most of the upper front of the moccasin. This style was preferred by the Menomini. The second variation had a much smaller vamp, also puckered, but with a central seam running from the top of the toe to the vamp. This type is often referred to as the Chippewa style because of its popularity with that tribe. The second basic style also was constructed from one piece of buckskin, but with a central puckered seam running down the upper front. This was the oldest style worn by both Forest and Prairie tribes and can be considered the fundamental Woodland style. Although this was the basic style, the moccasins of the Prairie tribes were distinguished by the cuffs, which flare diagonally outward at the front. The cuffs, or flaps as the Indians prefer to call them, were added as two separate pieces, each piece having a different beadwork or ribbonwork design on a single moccasin. Among all Woodland Indians, both sexes wore the same tribal style of moccasin, except for the Winnebago, who had one type with a square front flap that was worn only by the women.

Buckskin robes were worn in cold weather. There are early historical records of buckskin shirts, some of which were dyed brown with butternut juice, but these, most likely, were the result of white influence.

There were three styles of headdress. At times, colorful yarn sashes were wound around the head in turban-like fashion, and feathers were often added. On ceremonial occasions, turbans of otter hide were worn.

← *Modern dance costume. Chippewa.*

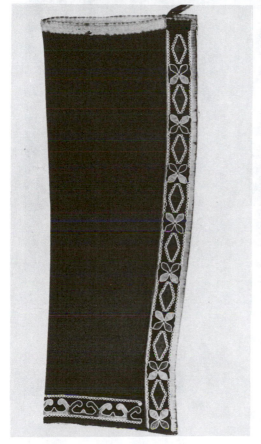

Chippewa male attire.

Example of early-style legging. Chippewa.

Two types of fur turbans. Menomini.

In one style, the whole otter skin was used, the head being brought around in a circle and then wedged in the animal's anus, while the tail flapped out on one side. These were sometimes decorated with beads and ribbons, and worn with eagle plumes. Also upon ceremonial occasions, particularly in times of war, a roach was worn. This was a crest of animal hair set on top of the head. Rows of the shorter, tail hair of the deer, dyed red, were combined with rows of the longer, white hair of the porcupine. Moose hair could replace deer hair, and, in the prairie area, where porcupines were not found, turkey beards were substituted for porcupine hair. A bone "roach spreader" ran through the top center of the headdress and forced the stiff hair upward and outward to give it a brushlike effect. It was embellished with a single eagle feather, the quill end swiveling in a bone socket attached to the center of the roach, and the feather swung freely as the man moved. Among the Sauk, the warrior's head was plucked free of all hair except at the top center, where a scalp lock was left; this measured about an inch and a half in diameter and six inches in length. This lock was then pushed through a hole in the roach and securely tied. It was more common, however, to draw a lock of hair from the crown through the hole in the roach, and tie it. In recent times, the roach was held on the head by a headband mount made of strap leather. In any case, it was worn with the crest beginning several inches back from the forehead, and it continued down the back of the head to the shoulders. The roach itself was con- structed on a bow loom. Small bundles of hair were doubled over a cord and tied. The cord then was spiraled around a central opening and sewn together as it was coiled. When it was not being worn, the roach was folded carefully and wrapped over a cylindrical stick.

Women's Clothing

The basic garment for the Forest woman was a sleeveless dress made of two deerskins, one for the front and one for the back, sewn together at the shoulders and belted. This was worn over an undershirt of woven nettle fiber. Buckskin leggings fell from the knees to the ankle and were fastened just below the knee with a thong or band. Moccasins completed the costume. For work, especially in warm weather, a tanned buckskin shirt sufficed. The long, full buckskin dresses, reaching to the ankles, with fringed sleeves and fringe at the bottom, were a relatively recent innovation simulating the white woman's dress of the late nine- teenth century. Among the Prairie women the skirt, rather than the full dress, was traditional.

In postcontact times, broadcloth became the prime material for the woman's costume, except among the Chippewa. Originally the skirt consisted of a square piece of buckskin, but in postcontact times broad- cloth was wrapped around the body, meeting in the front. The ends were

decorated with borders of silk applique or beadwork. The upper portion was folded outward over a belt. A second piece of applique'd or beaded broadcloth was worn, like a cape, over the shoulders. Broadcloth leggings with applique'd or beaded borders reached from the knee to the ankle. The moccasins, however, were still made of the traditional buckskin decorated with beads or ribbonwork.

Women wore their hair in a single braid falling down their backs. In historic times ribbons were often intertwined in the braid, and a comb of German silver was added for further decoration. Upon dress occasions, the older style of hair decoration was the "hair-tie." The braid was doubled up and tied in a "club." Around this was wound a strip of buckskin or cloth, about five by ten inches, each end decorated with quillwork or beadwork. To this hair-tie, long, narrow streamers of quillwork or loomed beadwork were attached, which hung nearly to the ground.

House Types

A variety of dwellings were used, according to the season. The most common was the dome-shaped wigwam, which served from late fall, through the winter, and well into the spring. With the exception of the Iroquois, all Woodland tribes from New England to the Mississippi River built this style of structure. The floor pattern was circular or, more commonly, oval. Saplings of an inch or more in diameter were cut and sharpened at the large end. Beginning at the doorway, these were set into the ground vertically and spaced about two feet apart. One pole and its opposite were bent toward the center to form an arch, and the ends were tied together with basswood-bark strips. When all the vertical poles were tied, other saplings were tied on horizontally, high enough to accommo-date the width of the cattail mats. More saplings were added to the top portion to form a sturdy framework. Then, beginning at the doorway, a mat was unrolled along the base, and its upper edge tied to the first horizontal pole. Other mats were added to cover the circumference of the framework. The Prairie tribes added more mats until all was covered except for a smoke hole and a doorway. The Forest tribes, living in birch country, utilized birchbark panels to cover the upper portion of the wigwam, the bark having been sewn together in strips about two by six feet. The cattail mats, prepared during the summer, and the birchbark strips, prepared in the spring, were rolled up and transported to the living site. Only the poles had to be prepared at the site. In some instances, the framework was covered with sheets of elm, ash, or cedar bark.

Inside the wigwam there was a central fireplace, and along the sides were arrangements for sleeping. The Prairie tribes slept on mats of grass and skins on the ground, while the Forest tribes constructed sleeping

Summer house. Menomini.

Birchbark wigwam. Chippewa.

60

Wood and Bark

Besides providing the Indian his fuel, housebuilding materials, and medicines, the forest gave him a rich variety of woods. Men did the woodworking and produced a host of crafted products: hunting and fishing equipment, household utensils, transportational devices, games, musical instruments, and other miscellany.

Tools and the techniques for using them included: stone (later steel) axes for chopping; wooden wedges for splitting; chisels, gouges, and knives for shaping; and scrapers for smoothing. The technique of bending wood without breaking it was well developed and was exploited in making canoe ribs, snowshoe frames, basket handles, lacrosse rackets, and other curved items. Another technique was the reduction by fire; for example, log mortars and dugouts were hallowed out by burning.

Bows and arrows were the primary implements in both hunting and warfare. The bow was the simple "flat" bow made of well-seasoned hickory, preferably, or of ash, or, occasionally, of elm, hemlock, or white oak. It was about four feet long, two inches wide at the center, tapering off toward each end, and rectangular in cross section. A popular form of decoration was a scallop design carved along one edge of the lower limb and along the opposite edge of the upper limb. When the tree was felled, a block larger than bow size was removed, careful account being taken of the grain of the wood. This was shaped to finished size with a crooked knife, smoothed with a scraper, and left to season. The Menomini rubbed theirs with bear grease right after the smoothing operation. Bowstrings were made of sinew, nettle fiber, or the skin from the neck of the snapping turtle.

The arrow shaft was made from cedar or pine. It was fletched with three sections of eagle, hawk, or turkey feathers, often dyed and then tied on with sinew. The most common tip was a chipped-stone, side-notched point tied on with sinew, but bone and antler were also used. The Menomini and the Chippewa had a special arrow for use in battle, one tipped with the spikelike claw of the turtle, for they believed that additional power was derived from the turtle spirit. Arrows with a knobbed or blunted end were used to hunt small game. When the Europeans arrived, iron tips soon replaced the traditional ones.

Spears with wooden shafts and single points were used for spearing the huge sturgeon, whereas a trident or three-pronged tip was used for smaller fish. Fish lures carved to simulate minnows and frogs were popular for ice fishing.

From the burled sections of such hardwoods as maple, birch, and elm, the men carved household utensils of simple beauty. Before the advent of the steel crooked knife, these had all been shaped by charring and scraping with stone and bone tools. Spoon handles were often ornamented with carved designs, and some, along with the bowls, bore carved effigies. Each person possessed his own spoon and bowl, which he carried to the feast, and food was transferred, with a large ladle, from the common cooking pot to each individual bowl.

Mortars were hallowed out of a log, and in these the shelled corn was pounded into meal with a double-ended pestle.

Winter transportation involved the use of the toboggan and, in later times, the sled. The toboggan was fashioned of two hardwood boards held together by cleats and turned up at the front end. The toboggans were narrow, little more than a foot wide, and ordinarily measured seven to ten feet in length. They were pulled by means of a strap across the man's chest or by three dogs, which were harnessed in single file because the paths through the forest were so narrow. Shorter toboggans were carried on the backs of hunters to transport game.

The sled was constructed of two strips of ash bent into a U shape and held to this form by struts. The lower half served as runners and the upper portion was joined by cross pieces, which created a platform. Some sleds had runners as separate pieces. Sleds made it easier to haul firewood and household burdens, and they were particularly valuable in the maple-sugar camps.

Snowshoes were indispensable to the men on their long winter hunts in the deep snows. The most common type consisted of a strip of green ash that had been bent, either over a fire or in hot water, to form a rounded front end. The ends were tied together at the rear. The Menomini called this type "catfish" because of its shape. Ordinarily, two crossbars were added for strength, and every other section was filled in with rawhide thongs, woven hexagonally with a center-eyed needle made of either wood or bone. A strip of leather across the wearer's instep held the snowshoe on his foot, and another strip was placed loosely around his heel. The Winnebago style of "catfish" was characterized by the "handle," the frame strip at the rear that, instead of being bound together all the way to the end, was left unbound about six inches from the end. A second type was similar to these, except for an upcurving front end. A double-pointed variety was made of two ash strips bound together at both ends. The women favored a smaller, oval-shaped style called "bear paw," rather crude, with a basswood-bark netting over a hastily prepared frame of branches.

Snowshoes were invented by the North American Indian, originating either among the Woodland Indians or in the Canadian subarctic area. The Prairie tribes lacked the toboggan, sled, snowshoes, and birchbark canoe, although it is probable that those who occupied the forest in previous times had once had them.

When the waterways were not frozen, transportation was made easier with dugouts and birchbark canoes. Dugouts were shaped and hollowed from logs, making them somewhat heavy, crude, and clumsy. The birchbark canoe, on the other hand, was light, graceful in design, and

Snowshoes. Chippewa.

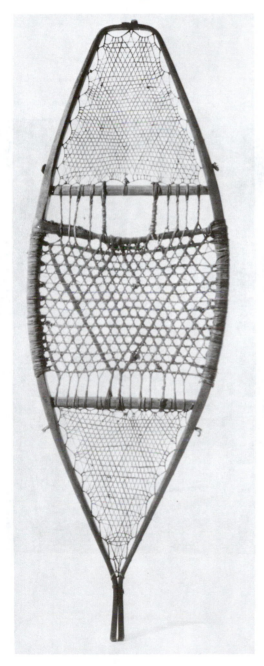

Building a birchbark canoe.

very maneuverable. All the Forest tribes of the Great Lakes region used birchbark canoes, but not those Prairie tribes who lived south of the whitebirch zone, the southern limits of which run through southern Minnesota, the northern two thirds of Wisconsin and Michigan, upper New York, and southern Massachusetts.

The thickness of the bark determined its use. Bark peeled in the spring was heavier and of a strength best suited for canoes, while that peeled in the summer was thinner and considered adequate for mats, containers, and other articles. Ordinarily bark was removed without injuring the tree, but in order to obtain the large sheets needed for canoes, the tree was felled. Canoe materials included the bark from the white birch for the covering, and white cedar for the "skeleton": the ribs, gunwales, thwarts, prow pieces, and flooring. The sewing elements were prepared from the roots of the spruce, the tamarack, or the jack pine. The long, shallow roots were grubbed out, brought to the camp, and soaked in water, then split and trimmed.

After the tree had been felled, an incision was made along one side so the bark could be pried off with a pole. At the construction site it was laid on the ground with the outer bark facing up. A canoe form was placed on the bark, which was weighted down with rocks, while the two sides of the bark were held upwards by means of posts driven into the ground. Cedar trees were split by maul and wedge, cut to suitable lengths for the various parts of the skeleton, and brought to the construction site for final shaping and trimming. A pair of gunwales were sewn onto the upper sides, and a curved prow piece was sewn into each end. Three or more thwarts were fitted into slots in the inboard side of each gunwale and sewn into place. The sewing was done with the aid of a slightly curved bone awl. The rib pieces were shaped with a crooked knife and soaked in water for a few days. Then they were dipped into hot water, bent in pairs into a U shape, and positioned in the canoe to set. When dry, they were removed, and thin floor boards were laid, shinglewise, in the bottom of the canoe. The ribs were replaced over the floor boards, the rib ends fitting between the gunwales. White pine pitch, to which charcoal had been added for coloring, was boiled and then applied to those places on the exterior that required sealing. These seams were then smoothed and cemented with the aid of a birchbark torch.

The canoe was propelled with cedar paddles, the paddler kneeling on the floor. Since the weight was a hundred pounds or less, it was easy to portage between lakes and streams. The Indians found it practical for hunting, fishing, collecting wild rice, and in historic times, fur trading. The white fur traders adopted it as a mode of transportation, the French voyageurs, for example, using birchbark canoes forty feet long and as wide as six feet to transport trade goods. The Woodland canoe was the prototype of the canoe used today by sportsmen in North America.

In addition to the canoes, birchbark was ingeniously fabricated into containers, mats, *Mide'* scrolls, moosecalls and, as a medium of pure art, dental pictographs (explained below).

Containers were devised by first heating the bark over a fire or steaming it to make it pliable, then bending it into the desired shape and sewing it with basswood fiber or spruce roots. For cooking, it was necessary that the container be watertight, and this was accomplished by dampening it, putting liquid in it before placing the vessel over the fire. Hot stones sometimes were added to make the food boil. Bark buckets served to catch dripping maple sap, which was then poured into larger buckets and carried to the boiling site. There also were birchbark vessels, *makuks,* which would not hold water. These were shaped like truncated pyramids and were used for storing maple sugar and wild rice as well as for gathering wild fruits and berries. There were large, shallow birchbark trays for winnowing wild rice. In more recent times, beautiful trinket boxes were made from birchbark; these were circular and square, with covers, and decorated with porcupine quills.

Mats, fashioned by overlapping sections of birchbark and sewing them together, were used to roof the wigwams and to hold wild rice when it was spread out to dry. Smaller panels of birchbark were sewn together and engraved with a pointed instrument, these designs and pictures serving as memory aids to the priests in the Medicine Dance rituals. For storing, they were easily rolled up into scrolls.

Smaller pieces of birchbark were shaped into cones and used as moosecalls to attract those animals during the hunt. Bark was tightly rolled into a torch and lighted, providing light for the camp, for nighttime fishing, and for shining deer. These also were the torches used to help flow the pitch into canoe seams. Except for making canoes and *Mide'* scrolls, gathering birchbark and fabricating it was done by women.

Dental pictographs were an art form unique to the Chippewa. A thin sheet of birchbark was folded in two and designs bitten into it with the canine teeth. When it was unfolded, it had a mirror pattern and was enjoyed as pure art. Designs, also, were added to the *makuks* by outlining a figure or sketch and then scraping away the background to expose the lighter shade.

String was manufactured from the inner bark of elm, cedar, and, particularly, basswood. The bark was peeled from the tree in long strips, preferably in the spring. The outer bark was taken off with the fingers or teeth, the inner bark then tied in coils and taken home. There, the narrow strips, which had been split, were used with no further preparation to bind together the pole framework of the wigwam.

Before making the string, the coils were boiled in a solution of wood-ash lye until the fibers began to separate. They were allowed to dry, then were cut into lengths of about three feet and the fibers completely separated by rasping the strip through a hole in the pelvic bone of a deer. The woman would hold two strands in one hand, place them on her bare

Dental pictographs.

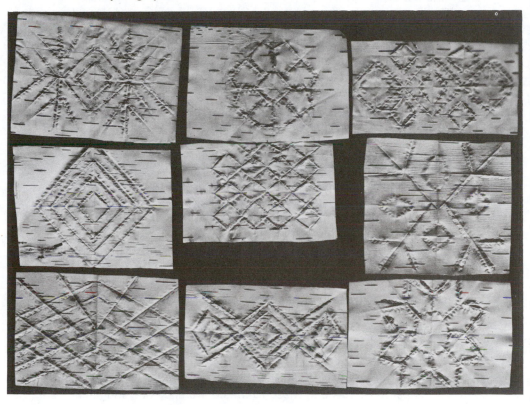

shin or thigh and, with the palm of the other hand, roll the fibers back and forth, twisting them into a string. A second pair of fibers were then laid over the combed ends of the first and rolled together, forming an invisible splice. As the twine grew, it was wound into a ball. When she had completed the prepared amount, the woman pulled the entire length of twine through the rasp once more, then rewound it into a ball to be stored. The twine was extremely strong, and the Indians found it useful in sewing cattail mats, weaving bulrush mats, weaving yarn and basswood storage bags, lashing together various parts of their wigwams, and tying wild rice before the harvest.

Kinnikinnick, a term from either the Chippewa or the Cree dialect of the Algonkian family of languages, literally means "what is mixed," and it refers to certain plant materials the Indians mixed with tobacco for smoking. The use of kinnikinnick was widespread among the Indians of North America, although the ingredients varied from area to area. In the Woodland region the favorite ingredients were the inner bark of certain willows and dogwoods, or sumac leaves. The Indians of California mixed dried manzanita leaves with tobacco, while the Blackfoot Indians of Montana used the leaves of the bearberry. Whatever plant was used, it nearly always dominated the final mixture, which ordinarily contained only about one third tobacco. Some Wisconsin Indians, especially the older ones, still prefer kinnikinnick to the straight pipe tobacco.

The method of preparation was simple: A man carefully selected red osier dogwood stems, cut them, and carried them back to the wigwam, where he scraped off the outer bark with a pocket knife. With the back of the same blade, he then scraped curlicues of the inner bark from the stem, and allowed them to fall on a cloth he had placed over his lap. It was this portion of the plant that he used. He made a drying rack by splitting one of the peeled stems halfway down and opening the end to form a Y. The opened portion he crisscrossed with other split stems to form a grid, and on this he placed the curlicues of inner bark. He forced the rack into the ground diagonally, just above a low fire, so that the bark was about a foot above the flames and could dry in the heat without being burned. In about twenty minutes the bark was toasted and crisp, so that, when he rubbed it between his palms, it was pulverized to the consistency of a rough-cut tobacco.

Why did the Indians use kinnikinnick? No one really knows, but one theory suggests an economic reason: the shortage of tobacco led to the addition of local plant materials to make the supply go further. A more plausible explanation, inasmuch as tobacco was abundant and easily raised in much of the Woodland area, seems to be that the Indians made use of the native, semiwild tobacco plant and did not process or age the leaves. The result was a rather strong, rank smoke when kinnikinnick was not mixed with it.

Quillwork

Quillwork was an ancient art of the Woodland Indian woman, and nowhere outside North America was porcupine quillwork found. Dyed porcupine quills were sewn with sinew onto buckskin clothing, knife sheaths, and medicine bags; woven on looms; or self-stitched on birch-bark boxes in designs both geometrical and floral. The quills were dyed with native vegetable dyes. They were moistened in the mouth and flattened by being pulled out between the teeth or with special bone flatteners. Then they were embroidered onto the buckskin with the sinew thread crossing over the quill; never through it: the quill would split. Before decorating the birchbark boxes, the woman soaked the quills in water until they were soft, left them unflattened, and then inserted the points through the awl-holes in the bark. The points were trimmed and bent back against the bark to hold them in place. Both floral and geometric designs were worked in this fashion. Quills were also woven on looms to make belts, tumplines, and decorative strips that were later applied to clothing. Pipestems were wrapped or bound with quillwork. Perhaps the finest woven quillwork or quilled loom work was done by the western Cree, who moved out to the northern Plains in historic times.

Beadwork

When the Europeans introduced glass beads the Woodland Indians switched from quill to bead embroidery. They excelled in beadwork, their finest art form.

As with the quillwork, beadwork lay in the woman's domain. She used both loom and embroidery techniques. The earliest loom was the bow loom, a bent stick with doubled-up birchbark heddles attached to each end to hold the sinew warp threads in place. The box loom was also used, a rectangular frame with the warp threads strung over the end bars. In historic times the beads were strung on silk or linen thread with a long, fine, steel needle. The end of the weft thread was tied to the left side of the warp threads and strung with the appropriate number of beads to fill one row of the warp. The string of beads was then passed under the warp threads from the left, and each bead was pushed up between the two warp threads. The beads were held in place with the left hand, the weft thread passing from right to left over the warp threads so that another row of beads was ready to be strung. By this method the Woodland women produced belts, garters, headbands, necklaces, and decorative bands to be fastened onto buckskin or cloth. The square weave was also produced with the aid of a wooden heddle. Heddle weaving resulted in the beadwork being woven with a double warp—a different technique, although the results look much the same as loom work.

Box loom and bow loom.

Quill-decorated birchbark boxes. Menomini and Chippewa.

Loom work. Menomini.

For embroidery, the "spot," or "overlay," stitch was used. Beads were strung on a thread and laid in position on the cloth or hide, with a second thread crossing over the first, usually after two or three beads, and then passed through or into the hide to hold the beads firmly in place. The earlier embroidery was done with sinew from either the deer or moose and, since it was not desirable for any stitches to show on the reverse side, the sinew was not passed entirely through the buckskin. Bead embroidery became popular on clothing and on the famous bandolier bags, which were worn as decorative accouterments on dress occasions. The latter were apparently derived from the bandolier or bullet pouch worn over one shoulder by the United States military. The Indians, however, never used them as carrying devices; some, in fact, were made with the pouch sewn shut. To a degree, they were a symbol of wealth, and an individual might wear as many as a dozen, although one or two was the usual number.

The antiquity of the floral designs so characteristic of Woodland decorative art, the leaves and flowers, has been open to question; some scholars believe the early Europeans, particularly the French, introduced them. Quilled floral designs appeared on medicine bags approximately two hundred years ago. It seems likely that these Indians, with their commitment to a forest ecology, would not ignore floral motifs and that some kind of floral design was used in precontact times. Their geometrical designs are certainly old, and the Woodland Indians had a penchant for a particular style of whitebead border called "otter tail."

While loom work is difficult to distinguish from tribe to tribe, embroidery has variations and distinctive traits, which aid in identification. For example, the embroidered work of the Forest tribes as compared to that of the Prairie tribes was always more realistic, usually to the extent that the leaves and flowers can be identified as to species, even including such details as veining and ribbing. The Prairie groups were less concerned with naturalism—in fact, stylization was the vogue. They emphasized such elements as bilateral symmetry, the outlining of a design with beads of another color—usually white, greater use of geometrical designs, and a predilection for solid designs rather than the unfilled-in, outline patterns that were quite common among the Forest tribes. When filled-in designs were done by the Forest tribes, the design was first outlined with a row of beads. This was also done by the Prairie groups, but the filled-in rows followed the curved contour of the outline rather than the Prairie preference for straight-row fill-in. In general, a bolder effect was created by the embroidery of the Prairie tribes.

On the whole, the Forest tribes adhered to a realistic treatment of floral patterns to the extent that the design elements usually can be identified as to the species of leaf or flower, although the combinations of these—oak leaves, grapes, and wild roses on one stem—are anything but realistic. The Prairie tribes, on the other hand, leaned more toward conventionalized designs and less internal detail.

Bandolier bag. Sauk.

Silk Applique'

Silk applique', or "ribbonwork," is another art form extremely important to the Woodland Indians. They cut patterns from silk and sewed them
as decoration onto cloth garments. Silk applique' was practiced, especially
by the Indians of the Great Lakes region and the Mississippi Valley,
perhaps as early as 1750. The Prairie Potawatomi, Miami, Kickapoo,
Sauk, and Fox were the most skillful in this art, with the Forest Potawatomi, Menomini, and Winnebago close behind. The northernmost tribes,
the Chippewa and Ottawa, had only rudimentary ribbonwork.

The earliest work was done with silk ribbon. While ribbonwork was
found mostly on women's dresses, it was occasionally used to decorate
men's leggings, moccasins, and cradle-board wrappers. Although geometrical designs were used to a considerable extent, the majority were floral.
In very recent times bolt silk, nylon, and rayon were used: the women cut
designs with scissors from one color of silk, sewed them onto a panel of
another color, and then sewed this, as a decorative border, to a broadcloth garment. Silk was applique'd to buckskin, but this was rare.

Women sometimes sewed the design down with silk thread in a color
that contrasted to that of the pattern. This was particularly effective in the
cross-stitch, which resulted in an X-shaped thread pattern, and in the
herringbone stitch. The blind stitch, one in which the threads are hidden,
was used to sew the panel onto the broadcloth; later, the panels were
stitched on with the sewing machine. Today, silk applique' is a dying art.

Weaving

"It is truly astonishing," wrote Skinner, "that the ability of the
Woodland tribes in the matter of textile arts has been so little recognized
by students" (1921, p. 230). This ingenuity is well demonstrated by the
kind and variety of woven articles: fiber and yarn bags, sashes and garters,
rush and bark mats.

Bags for carrying and storing sacred objects and household goods
were woven of basswood and other bast-fiber string, nettle fiber, and
buffalo wool, though in later times commercial yarn was used. Twining
was the technique used for yarn bags; this was done with a warp suspended between two thick, springy sticks set vertically in the ground. The
weaving proceeded downward. A pair of colored yarn weft strands were
twined around one, or often two, warp strands until a row around the
entire bag had been completed. On the earlier bags rows of zoomorphic
designs were common. Thunderbirds, spirits in panther form, as well as
humans, were interspersed with bands of geometrical motifs, and one side
was apt to show a different set from the other. On more recent bags, the
designs show a concentration of bands of floral and geometric patterns.

Silk applique'. Menomini.

Yarn bag weaving. Chippewa.

Woven bags. Menomini, Chippewa, and Potawatomi.

Weaving a yarn sash. Chippewa.

Storage bags and carrying bags of similar size and of a rectangular shape were also made of basswood. The inner bark of basswood was boiled, then pulled into untwisted strands and dyed, after which the strands were placed over a crossbar so that they hung down in equal lengths on each side. A pair of twisted basswood cords were twined around one or two warp strands in rows about a half inch apart. The warp strands were grouped by color, which resulted in a design of vertical colored bands.

Hulling bags were woven of cedar bark in an open, twine weave. These bags held corn while it was being soaked for cleansing after it had been boiled in an ash lye to loosen the hulls from the kernels.

Sashes and garters were woven of commercial yarn in three or more colors, a favorite being deep red. Finger weaving was a popular technique, in which the yarn strands were wound around a short stick in parallel rows and interlaced with one another. The one set of strands served as both warp and weft. The weaving progressed downward. Netting and braiding techniques were also used to make yarn sashes and garters. Women wore sashes around the waist as decorative belts to hold their dresses in place. The men wore them around the waist for decoration or to keep a buckskin jacket closed, but occasionally one was worn over the shoulder or wound around the head in turban fashion. Garters were worn just below the knee, by both men and women, to support the leggings.

Of the woven mats, those made of bulrushes were the most common. They served as floor coverings and house partitions or were laid on the ground or floor for serving food, especially at the feasts. The bulrushes were gathered in early summer, bleached, dried, and dyed. The ends of the rushes were braided to form an even edge and then hung from a crossbar between two posts set in the ground. A basswood cord weft was passed from left to right with the rushes twined around it. The weft rows were about a half inch apart, and the weaving progressed from top to bottom. A braided edge finished it off. The designs were geometrical, but zoomorphic motifs, particularly the thunderbird, appeared on smaller mats that served as wrappers for war bundles.

Where bulrushes were scarce, a similar kind of mat was woven from the inner bark of red cedar. This was gathered in May or June, and split, for both warp and weft, into thin strips about a quarter inch wide. The weaving was done on a frame that resembled the one used for the bulrush mats, but the technique was a simple over-and-under, or checkerwork, weave. Storage bags also were woven from the same kind of cedar strip and by the checkerwork technique.

Another type of mat was fabricated of cattails, but sewn, rather than woven, and used as a wigwam covering. The cattails were gathered in the fall, trimmed and carried home, where they were laid out to dry in the sun. The outer layer of each stalk was peeled off. The stalks were cut to even lengths and then laid parallel on a level stretch of ground, their ends

Sewing cattail mat. Mexican Kickapoo.

Sewing cattail mat, detail. Mexican Kickapoo.

alternately reversed. The ends of one edge were braided over a basswood cord. Another cord was threaded through a hole near the center of a curved mat-needle. This needle, a foot long, was made from the rib of either a buffalo or a cow. The needle was passed through the stalks, across the mat, at intervals of about six inches. From time to time, water was sprinkled on the stalks to keep them pliable, as was the case with all mat weaving. When the sewing was completed, the ends were braided over a cord. The mat was rolled up and stored until needed. Among the Forest tribes the lower third of the wigwam was mat-covered, the remaining portion being spread with birchbark. The Prairie groups, to whom birchbark was not available, covered the entire wigwam with mats that were often twice the size of those used by the Forest peoples.

Baskets

Among the Forest peoples birchbark containers were more extensively used than baskets, although all Woodland groups had some form of basketry. One of the most ancient and widespread was the coiled basket made of sweet grass, *Torresia odorata Hitchc.*, which exudes a fragrant odor, particularly when dried. The grass, which grows about two feet high, was bundled into coils about an eighth to a quarter inch in diameter. One end was knotted, and the coil was wound around the knot; it was fastened by being sewn with a fiber thread. When the flat base was completed, the sides were built up in a bowl form. The only implement used was a bone awl to open a hole for the passage of the thread, which was passed around the free coil and beneath the fastened coil below. Besides the round and oval bowl forms, there were trinket baskets and shallow dishes and trays.

Wicker baskets of willow stems, cedar roots, or basswood bark were also constructed, but to a limited degree.

It is very likely that the plaited, black-ash splint baskets were, as Skinner (1921, p. 293) suggests, a relatively recent development, for these baskets were introduced by the Oneida and Stockbridge when they moved into Wisconsin in the 1820s. The Winnebago, particularly, have been active in producing this type of basket.

Hide Preparation

This description is based specifically on the methods used by the Chippewa, but the process was similar among the other Woodland groups.

After a deer had been shot, the entrails were removed and the cavity stuffed with grass. The hunter transported the deer home, on his back, with the aid of a tumpline made from a hide strap about a foot long and two to three inches wide. To each end was attached a leather thong three to four feet long. Half of one thong was passed around a stick inserted under the deer's breastbone, and with the other half the hunter tied the four feet together. Half of the other thong was passed around another stick, which had been inserted under the pelvis, at the pubic symphysis. By passing the thong through two cuts made in the cheek and pulling the head back towards the body, the hunter bound the animal's head to its side. Then he pulled on the central strap, placed it around his forehead, and slung the deer onto his back, firmly anchoring it just above the small of his back. He packed it home to skin it the following morning.

To remove the skin, the cut in the abdomen was extended back to the anus, forward past the breastbone, and up the underside of the neck to the head. The skin was pulled away from the flesh with the left hand, while the right fist made a punching motion to further separate it; a knife was never used in this process because of the possibility of cutting the hide and spoiling it. After the hide was pulled away from the underside, a circular cut was made around each leg, about a foot from the toe end. From this cut another one was made down the inside of each leg to join the ventral cut. Then the skin was pulled off the four legs, the carcass rolled over on one side, and the hide pulled off the upturned side. It was rolled over to the other side and the hide pulled off the remaining part of the body, then off the neck up to the head. The final cut was made starting from the ventral one on the neck and going up and around the head on each side, meeting on top of the head near the antlers; then the hide was pulled free.

Now the woman took over the tanning process. If the hide was to be tanned within a day or two, it was put into a tub of water and left to soak. Otherwise, the blood and dirt were rinsed off and it was hung on a clothesline or a branch, skin side out, where it dried and stiffened. The former was referred to as a "green" hide and the latter as a "dried" hide; it was the green hide that was preferred by the tanners. Since tanning was woman's work, nearly all the women and their daughters were equipped with the proper tools and had been taught the technique at an early age.

Before it could be tanned, it was necessary to soften a dried hide by soaking it in water for at least two days. This was not essential, of course, with a green hide. The hide was washed with soap in lukewarm water to remove dirt, blood, and other extraneous material. It was then thoroughly rinsed, wrung out, and thrown over a beaming post, a peeled log about eight inches in diameter and three to four feet long; this log was either set into the ground at a forty-five-degree angle or held in that position by two legs. In historical times, the beaming tool or scraper was a cylindrical piece of wood, usually cedar, a foot and a half long and two and a half inches in diameter. Into this was imbedded the blade of a common "silver" table knife, the edge of which had been filed flat so that the hide would not be cut while it was being scraped. At prehistoric sites archaeologists have found beaming tools of bone with slots in them for the insertion of chipped-stone scrapers. The woman stood leaning over the high end of the beaming post. She held the beamer in both hands, the blade pointing slightly backward, and, with each downward push, she scraped a path of hair. A winter hide sometimes required shearing off some of the thick hair before scraping could proceed. When all the hair and scarfskin was removed, the hide was reversed and the skin side scraped to remove excess bits of flesh. The hide was washed again with soap and water, then rinsed. In order to wring out the water thoroughly, the woman made a loop of the hide around an upright post, inserted a stick through the loop, and, leaning heavily on the stick, twisted it so that the pressure on the hide removed all the water.

The next step was an important one, for it softened the hide considerably. The hide was thoroughly soaked in a tub of warm water that contained dried deer brains. These had been prepared by being placed, when fresh, in a frying pan of boiling water and allowed to set for about ten minutes. When they turned from gray to white, the brains were taken out, allowed to dry in the house, and then wrapped in a cloth or buckskin for future use. When dried in this manner, they were tan in color. Although any animal brains, such as beaver, rabbit, or pig, could be used, the brains of deer were by far the most common. If brains were not available, the white of eggs could be substituted. After the hide had been soaked in the brain solution for about five minutes, or even less, it was rinsed in clear water and wrung out by being twisted around the wrist. Further wringing was done by the stick-twisting method. A winter hide usually required another soaking in the brain solution.

The hide was then hung on a line, the wrinkles pulled out, and bullet holes sewn up with needle and thread. Along the edge of the hide, holes were cut at intervals of three to four inches and a cord was passed through one hole and out the next all the way around the skin; this permitted easy suspension on the stretching frame. Every tanner had one of these frames set up permanently in a shady spot in her yard. It consisted merely of two posts set into the ground five to six feet apart, and, to form a rectangle, two poles were tied on, horizontally, about three and a half feet apart. A cord was attached to the neck of the hide and fastened to one of the upright posts of the frame. The tail portion was attached to the other upright, and the legs were tied with cords to each of the four corners of the frame. A long cord was passed through the edge lacing and then around the frame and the hide itself could be drawn taut within the rectangle. A stretching tool, now commonly made from an ax handle with the head end cut to a convex, blunt edge, was pushed with great force in a sweeping motion across the hide, causing it to stretch. After a few minutes of this, the suspension cords needed tightening. This process was repeated over and over until the hide had reached its maximum size, with a considerable gain in length and width. Intermittently during this process, any thick or hard spots, which usually were found on the skin side, were scraped so the hide would stretch evenly; this was done with an implement fashioned from a band of iron, with a rounded edge, which had been bent into a right angle.

During all this time the hide was drying. It was imperative that it be completely dry before it could be removed from the frame. The frame was always set up in the shade so the hide would not dry too rapidly; otherwise it would shrink and stiffen. Depending on the weather, the hide stayed on the frame for about an hour to an hour and a half. When the woman removed it, the hide was pure white and very soft to the touch.

Now the hide was ready to be smoked to a golden brown. The smoke helped to keep it from getting stiff when wet, and the color prevented it from too rapid soiling. The edges of the hide were sewn together to form a cylindrical bag with an opening at one end about a foot or more in diameter. Onto this end the woman sewed a strip of cloth about two feet wide that she fitted over the smudge bucket to prevent the lower put of the hide from getting soiled or burned. Then she hung the hide from the branch of a tree by a cord, so that the open end nearly reached the ground. When she did the smoking in her wigwam or a storage hut, as was usually the case since she wanted to keep it out of the wind, she suspended the bag from a top support. She started a smudge fire in a galvanized water pail, using rotten pine or poplar or, in some cases, dried Norway pine cones. When the smudge had a good start, she slipped the bucket under the bag. The strip of cloth around the bottom trapped the rising smoke inside the bag, smoking and coloring the inner side of the hide. More fuel was added at intervals. The smooth or hair side required about fifteen minutes, while the skin or rough side took approximately twenty minutes. If she wanted it darker, she smoked the hide a while longer. Finally a beautiful golden color, the hide was taken down, and, after the threads were cut, it was hung on a line to air out. It was now ready to be used.

A summer hide, although thinner, was tougher than a fall or winter hide, and the women preferred them for making clothing. The best hides were those taken in July and August. Winter hides were not so numerous because less hunting was done in the wintertime, for then the meat was lean and it tasted of winter forage. Early spring hides, especially those secured in April, could not be tanned because the hair was deep in the skin. In the old days, such hides were scraped on the skin side to remove excess flesh, dried, and used as rugs in the wigwams.

While buckskin was valued primarily for clothing, it also was utilized for thongs for cradle boards and snowshoes, storage bags for tobacco, and for the heads of several kinds of drums.

Silverwork

The art of silversmithing was introduced to the Indians along the Atlantic Coast by early European colonists. In time, it was taken up by nearly all the Woodland tribes. The early work was done in coin silver but was soon replaced by German silver, an alloy composed mostly of nickel, with some zinc and copper. Their gravers and dies for cutting and stamping designs were improvised from files. The silverworking set also included a small vise, hammer, pincers, compass, and soldering iron. The German silver was purchased in sheets and fashioned into circular brooches, bracelets, headbands, combs, rings, and earrings; these were then embellished with cutout designs or incised lines, dots, and figures. Brooches in great profusion often decorated the women's blouses and dresses. Silver inlay was applied to pipestems.

The only other metalwork known to have been done by the Woodland peoples was during precontact times, when a few items, such as awls and celts, were cold-hammered from native copper.

Woodland silverwork.

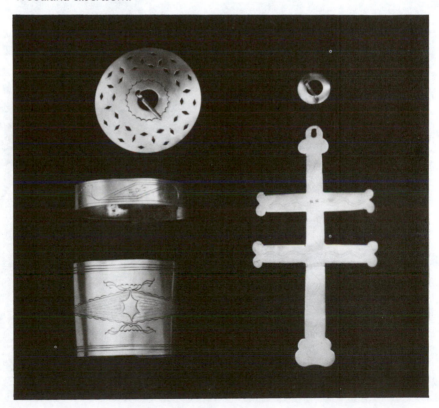

Drum (or Dream) Dance drum.

6

Religious and Ceremonial Life

The world of the Woodland Indian was filled with a host of spirits *(manido;* plural *manidog),* which inhabited trees, plants, birds, animals, and cosmic phenomena. Those of major importance were the sun, the moon, thunder, lightning, the four winds, and the thunderbirds, or eagles. Offerings of tobacco were being made constantly to protect the Indians' health, assure their safety in storms, plead for help from the *manidog,* or express their gratitude for past favors.

In addition to the benign spirits, their world was peopled with a throng of fearsome ones: ghosts, the Water Monster, and the *Windigo,* a cannibalistic giant who stalked the winter woods in search of people to devour. In another category there was the culture hero and demigod, *Wenebojo* (the Chippewa term; called *Manabush* by the Menomini, and by other names in other Algonkian dialects). His was the dual role of trickster and bringer of good things. It was he who taught the Indians about maize, tobacco, and medicinal plants, and his exploits form a major portion of Woodland mythology.

Also of primary value to the Indian was his guardian spirit, an especially helpful personal spirit acquired during the vision he experienced while fasting as a youth. The individual's spirit power was also significant, and certain people, particularly shamans and priests, were recognized as possessing spiritual power to an extraordinary extent. The shaman nearly always was the most feared and respected individual in the community, for he had power to produce both good and evil. Religion was primarily an individual affair with the Woodland Indian, and one that he practiced constantly. Organized group activities were comparatively rare.

Medicine Dance

The major religious ceremony, the Medicine Dance *(Midé'wiwin* in Chippewa) was held only once or twice a year. It is too complex, both in meaning and ritual, to describe adequately here, but the important elements can be summarized.

The *Mide'wiwin* (both Jones [1917] and Landes [1968] refer to it as a mystic rite) was the primary ceremony of the Medicine Lodge Society, to which membership was obtained by preliminary instruction and formal initiation. This was done at one of the semi-annual meetings held in late spring and early fall. The instructions and ceremony were under the leadership of a number of recognized priests who were often shamans; each of them had an assistant, or "runner." In late years, the ceremony lasted from two to seven or eight days, depending upon the number of candidates. It was held in a long, semicylindrical lodge that had been constructed for the purpose. The lodge was built the day before the ceremony began, or, if an old lodge was used, it was repaired then. It consisted of a pole framework that was left open, except for cedar boughs placed along the sides and up to a height of two or three feet. In former times, some tribes completely covered the Medicine Lodge.

A candidate for the ceremony was one who had been ill or who had dreamed that he should "go through" the *Mide'wiwin*. He held a feast to announce his intentions, to which he invited his friends and a *Mide'* priest. If the priest agreed that he must "go through," the candidate made the requisite preparations. He began by buying the blankets and pails needed for the initiation fee, which came to a considerable amount. The candidate then received a cowrie shell *(mi'gis)* on a thong, with the admonition that he was to wear it around his neck at all times until his initiation. During this period he also gave a series of feasts, to which his sponsors and the priest were invited.

The priests decided when and where the initiation ceremony would take place, and all the candidates were assembled after having received the invitational tobacco. In an ordinary-size wigwam built on the dance grounds, they were given secret preliminary instructions, were advised about their conduct during the ceremony, were informed about the ritual and told a portion of the origin tale, and were taught those songs, meanings, and secrets of the Society related to the "degrees" they were taking. They were also given a sweat bath.

On the first day of the public ceremony, the candidates' blankets and pails were hung on the ridgepole of the lodge. From the doorway at the east end, they were led into the lodge and seated in the center, where individual stakes had been driven into the ground. Then the members, led by a priest singing the entrance song, marched around the lodge carrying tobacco, food, and their medicine bags. Outside the east entrance they placed tobacco on a rock, then marched inside and took their seats along the perimeter of the wigwam.

The ceremony was directed by the priests, who did the speaking and the singing, and directed the dancing, the feasting, and the ritualistic maneuvers. The major ceremonial objects included the *mi'gis*, medicine bags, water drums, gourd rattles, and birchbark scrolls with incised characters, which served as mnemonic aids to the *Mide'* priests (see p.

120). An essential feature of the public initiation was the magical "shooting" of the shells into the bodies of the candidates. This highly dramatic ritual was performed by the sponsors. Holding high their medicine bags, they pointed them at the candidates; the *mi'gis*, full of a mystic vital force, would drive out the sickness and "renew life." The shell actually was dropped in front of the candidate, but he was to act as though he had been shot. During this procedure the initiate received a medicine bag, which was one of the following:

First Degree   mink, otter, muskrat, or beaver
Second Degree   owl or hawk
Third Degree   snake, fox, or wildcat claw
Fourth Degree   bear paw or cub bear

After the shooting, the initiates distributed their blankets and pails to the *Mide'* priests, the runners, and the sponsors. When all the candidates had been initiated, the atmosphere became more relaxed, and the members filed around the lodge, holding their medicine bags and "shooting" one another in a general melee. During this time there were sleight-of-hand tricks and other entertainment to impress the audience. The initiates were the last to leave, and they took with them their new medicine bags and the decorated stakes at which they had been seated.

At the time Robert Ritzenthaler worked with the Chippewa, the *Mide'wiwin* was so dominated by the curative aspect that sickness was actually a prerequisite for membership. When he discovered someone wearing the *mi'gis*, the shell that indicated he was to be initiated at the next ceremony, any question concerning his health was accepted as an appropriate one, and the details were supplied. In only one instance, among the twenty or so candidates he observed at four different ceremonies, was illness not the reason for his "going through." In this case a young man was being put through by proxy; he was taking the place of his stepfather, who was to have been initiated but who had died suddenly. This is quite a different situation from that described by Hoffman (1886, pp. 163-64) for the Minnesota Chippewa in the 1880s. He wrote that entrance into the *Mide'wiwin* was a routine and natural part of one's life, with the application for entrance the result of a dream, or, if the desire to join was not blessed by a dream, he simply told the *Mide'* priest that he wished to purchase a *mi'gis*. In the 1940s even babies who were, or had been, ill could be inducted into the Society, and that seems to have been another distinct departure from the old tradition. While curing, and prayers for health and new life, were certainly important elements in the old *Mide'wiwin*, they never dominated the ceremony so completely as in later years.

The curative function of the *Mide'wiwin* was based, primarily, on the supernatural, although practical techniques were not neglected. While it was formerly a significant feature of the *Midé'wiwin*, medicinal instruction has degenerated to an almost negligible element. At Lac Vieux Desert reserve in Michigan in the 1940s the *Midé'* priest insisted that the candidates were informed about only two medicines during the four degrees. This is quite different from the situation described by Kohl (1860, p. 382), who said that one Chippewa estimated he had traded forty packets of beaver skins for medical knowledge in the *Midé'wiwin* Society. Kohl figured the man had thus invested some $30,000 in his medical education.

Brave Dance

The Brave Dance, or Chief Dance, was a religious ritual in which the guardian spirits of a number of people were enlisted to assist one or more individuals or the entire community. Although it is now popularly called the Chief Dance by groups of the Wisconsin Chippewa, the Indian term, *ogicidá'nimidiwin*, is literally translated as "Brave Dance," in reference to an Indian warrior, and it was called the "War" Dance by some tribes. Originally, it was a ceremony held before a war party was sent out. A group of people entreated their guardian spirits to protect the warriors and to insure their success in battle.

The ceremonial pattern consisted of the invitation, tobacco (which was carried by a runner), and dedication of food and tobacco to the *manidog*. This was done by a speaker who was recognized for his ability and his rapport with the spirit world. Then came the feast, followed by singing and dancing to the rhythm of a tambourine drum. The participants voluntarily recited their war exploits and enlisted the aid of their own guardian spirits on behalf of the warriors. Recently the Wisconsin Chippewa held the Brave Dance primarily because a sick man dreamed that he should hold one in order to recover, or because someone dreamed that sickness was about to descend upon the community. At the gathering, which was held in a house rather than a wigwam, the people called upon their guardian spirits to dispel the sickness. The Brave Dance was held to ask protection for a young man going into the armed forces, to ask for a bountiful harvest, of wild rice for example, or to try to avert inclement weather such as a particularly severe winter.

Drum Dance

The nineteenth century saw the entrance of two other religious complexes, the Drum Dance and peyote, both of which moved in from the west and took root only in the Wisconsin/Minnesota area.

The Drum Dance, also called the Dream Dance and the Powwow, originated on the plains, and seems to have been based on the Omaha

Grass Dance. The story goes that a young Sioux girl had been trapped near her village after a battle between the Indians and some white soldiers. When she tried to flee with the others, she failed to keep up with them and hid in a nearby lake, hoping the white men would soon leave. But they stayed for six days (or ten days, according to one story); during which time she remained hidden by some lily pads, neither eating nor drinking. Finally she was taken up into the sky by the *manido,* who praised her for her courage. He then told her about the Dream Dance and how the ceremony should be conducted; that peace could be effected between all Indians and the white man if she persuaded her people to follow the ritual. He gave her certain ethical instructions, too. When she had her vision, she was sick and nearly dead, but when she awoke she was cured. The sacred drum became the central element in the ceremony of the "drum religion." Peace, good moral conduct, obedience to law, a sense of responsibility, and assisting one's fellow man were intrinsic values to be learned and upheld by the members. The Sioux presented a drum to the Minnesota Chippewa and taught them the rites; they in turn introduced the new religion to the Wisconsin Chippewa during the 1870s.

The ceremony itself revolved around a number of sacred drums made from wooden washtubs, each supported off the ground by means of four stakes. They were covered with calf hide and highly decorated with paint, beadwork, and other trappings, all of which were symbolical. An organization of members was attached to each drum, and they were spoken of as "belonging" to a certain drum, although the drum itself was owned by just two individuals. Each member had a particular place at the dance ring or around the drum, and there were specific duties for each one: speaker, singer, drum beater, pipe tender, and heater of the drum-head. The calumet, or peace pipe, was also an intrinsic part of the ceremony. Women could belong to a drum, but they had no explicit duties; they accompanied the men by humming, and they joined in the dancing.

At various times throughout the year, small home meetings were held for a drum, but the main ceremony was, ideally, a four-day event held twice a year—the magic number four recurs in Woodland ritual and ceremony as it does among all other American Indians. These gatherings generally followed the *Mide'wiwin.* All the drums in the band were assembled for the ceremony, which was held in a special lodge or in an outdoor square (originally it was a circle) surrounded by benches or low fencing. There were openings on two sides. It was expressly forbidden that dogs be allowed in the enclosure, and, in the early days, they were killed if they happened to wander in. At the ceremony the speakers thanked everyone for coming, and acknowledged the aid given the assembly by the drum spirit, particularly stressing all the virtues mentioned above. The major portion of the ceremony consisted of singing and dancing, the latter an individual affair, hopping first on one foot and then on the other in the same spot. Only designated members, seated around the drum in the center of the ring, did the singing and drumming. There were a great many songs to memorize, for each member had his own, and, when it was sung, according to a definite order, he would get up and dance; after that, others could join in. When his song was finished, the member contributed something, possibly a blanket, a gun, or an article of clothing, to a fellow member of his choice. If an invited representative from another settlement was present, a bundle of gifts was given to him also, for distribution to his people. He himself had brought an adequate number of presents to the hosts. This presentation of gifts was an indispensable feature of the dance.

The Drum Dance also was a sort of social clearinghouse for such events as marriage, divorce, and removal of mourning, but in recent years it has become essentially a social dance, in which singing, dancing, feasting, and visiting are the main attractions. However, prayers and invocations of prosperity, good health, and brotherhood still accompany the ceremony.

Peyote

The use of the spinless cactus mescal *(Lophophora williamsii)* as the basis of the peyote religion began with Indians living in western Mexico and spread up through the Plains area during the 1840s to 1880s. It was introduced into the western Woodlands by the Winnebago about 1908. From the Winnebago, who are still the chief advocates of the cult, it spread to the Forest Potawatomi, the Sauk and the Fox, and, to a lesser degree, the Menomini, while only feeble inroads were made among the Chippewa. Although most of the concepts and rituals centered on those of the Plains Indians, the Winnebago early introduced certain Christian elements. It is now a nationally organized religion, having been incorporated in 1918 as the Native American Church.

The Winnebago still hold nightlong meetings as regularly as possible (preferably on Saturday) and on such holidays as Memorial Day and Labor Day. However, a member can sponsor and schedule a meeting at any time. They assemble in a house or in a special large, canvas-covered tipi. A temporary altar is set up, and it is the shape of this altar, usually a mound of earth if the ceremony is in a tipi, from which the names of the predominant cults originated: either a Half Moon or a Cross Fire. Occasionally some of the Half Moon group will worship with the Cross Fire people, and vice versa. On the altar rests the "king" peyote (so called because of its size) and possibly a Christian bible and a fire. The officers sit in a prescribed arrangement at the altar, with the members around the periphery of the tipi, men on the inside and women on the outside of the circle. The leader will give invocations; then singing begins to the accompaniment of a water drum, which is passed around the circle and is especially reserved for this rite. Only the men do the singing, never the women, and each man sings four songs, in accordance with the old religious significance of the number four. A gourd rattle is passed, counterclockwise, to those who wish to sing the peyote songs. The peyote "buttons," four of them if there are enough, either are eaten by the participants or an infusion of tea is brewed from them and then this is drunk. Either of these induces visions in accentuated colors, and a decided feeling of euphoria and heightened awareness of the tactile and auditory senses. Apparently there are no deleterious aftereffects, and it is not considered habit-forming. It was and still is believed that peyote possesses medicinal qualities; sick people attend the regular rites, hoping to be cured, as well as the special ceremonies held for certain sick individuals. From time to time during the ceremonies a member gives voluntary testimonials of having been cured, or of having had a salutary vision or revelations. Peyote ceremonies are also held at the time of funeral rites. The meetings always conclude in the morning with a feast.

Christianity

Missionaries have been active in the Woodland area for over four hundred years, and, at the present time, the majority of the Indians are, at least nominally, Christian.

Bear Ceremonialism

The circumpolar trait of bear ceremonialism seeped down to the northern tribes. Especially among the Menomini, Chippewa, Ottawa, and Potawatomi the bear commanded considerable respect and played a substantial part in their religion, notably in the Medicine Dance.

After a hunter had killed a bear, the head, which had been liberally decorated with beadwork and ribbons, and the hide were laid out on a mat. A slice of the tongue was hung up for four days. The body was not chopped up, but carefully disjointed with a knife to show the respect with which the Indians regarded the animal. People were invited to the feast by the usual invitations of tobacco. Although other foods were provided, everyone also ate some of the bear meat. Food that a bear would like, including maple sugar and berries, was laid out for it. If it was a male, a fine, beaded man's costume was arranged next to the hide; if a female, a woman's costume was so placed.

During the feast, a speaker talked to the bear village, pointing out the excellent treatment the Indians had accorded the present visitor and that other bears would be similarly and respectfully welcomed. After the feast the bones were gathered up and piled together—never were they left scattered about.

Tobacco Ritual

Throughout all the rites, ceremonies, and religious observances of the Woodland Indians, tobacco was the unifying cord, the thread of communication between the human element and the spiritual powers. It was believed that the *manidog* were extremely fond of tobacco and that the only way they could get it was from the Indians, either by smoke from a pipe or by offerings of the dry tobacco itself. According to tradition, the Indians had received tobacco as a gift from *Wenebojo*, the culture hero, who had stolen it from a mountain giant and then given the seed to his brothers.

In nearly all facets of their lives the Indians had reason to solicit the spirits for acts of kindness or to render thanks for past favors. Dry tobacco was placed at the base of a tree or shrub from which medicine was being gathered, and a pinch was thrown in the water before each day's gathering of wild rice to assure a bountiful harvest. Before setting out in a canoe, a safe return was assured by throwing tobacco on the water. On any other journey or on a hunt, when the Indian encountered singular features of the landscape—waterfalls, misshapen trees, oddly shaped rocks, certain lakes or islands which were said to harbor spirits—he paused for a smoke and left a pinch of tobacco as an offering. When a storm was approaching, families protected themselves by placing a small amount of tobacco on a nearby rock or stump. Tobacco was placed at graves as an offering to the departed spirit. When someone asked an elder to relate a myth or a folktale, he accompanied the request with a gift of tobacco. Before all religious ceremonies, tobacco was offered to the spirits. The universal method of inviting one to a feast or notifying one of a ceremony was the delivery, by a runner, of a small amount of dry tobacco. Tobacco sealed peace treaties between tribes and agreements between individuals. When a shaman agreed to accept a client's case, he indicated it by taking the proffered gift of tobacco. Anyone who has done field work with these Indians has learned that tobacco was a most acceptable gift, involving a touch of reverence and mutual understanding.

Tobacco was consumed primarily in pipes and was smoked by both men and women, but not by the children. *Kinnikinnick* was added in varying amounts to give what they considered a better smoke. Smoking the pipe for ceremonial and offeratory reasons seems to have been about as common as smoking it for personal satisfaction.

Archaeological evidence suggests that the early forms were stone "pebble" pipes and elbow-shaped pipes of pottery. In historic times, the Siouan or calumet shape was preferred. The men carved these from stone, preferably catlinite, a reddish sedimentary rock found at Pipestone, Minnesota and in northern Wisconsin. The manufacture of pipes was the last vestige of stoneworking by the Woodland tribes.

Ceremonial pipes were usually equipped with a long wooden calumet stem, while those used daily had shorter stems. In the early days, the stem consisted of two halves, with the smoke hole carved out of the center. After metal was introduced, the smoke channel was burned from a single stem by the insertion of a hot wire or metal rod.

Ancient and modern calumets. Milwaukee Public Museum collection.

Shaman's puppets. Menomini.

7

Shamanism and Curative Techniques

Much of the curative function in traditional Woodland culture was delegated to the shaman or medicine man, a specialist recognized for his rapport with the supernatural. In both the Prairie and the Forest tribes there were two types of shamans, whose concerns were primarily those of healing, and a third, whose art seemed to lean toward the darker side. The first two, the conjuror or tent-shaker and the sucking doctor, enjoyed extremely high status in the band, and were, in fact, generally the most feared and respected persons in the community, for they possessed and often exercised the power to practice evil as well as good. The third one, the *Wa'beno* (literally Morning Star Man, in Menomini), derived his power from the morning star, a power that appears to have been more nefarious than benevolent. In the minds of the Woodland Indians, health and long life represented the highest good, and he who possesed knowledge conducive to that end was the most highly esteemed among them.

Shamans were male, with rare exceptions. Although their powers had been obtained during the vision quest, they remained latent until fairly late in life. Not until one had attained middle age or more could he actually practice, for it was said that, if a novice shaman began too early, he might forfeit his power or even his life.

Not infrequently an individual was both a conjuror and a sucking doctor. Of the two, the conjuror had the wider powers, for he not only could heal magically but also possessed a clairvoyant ability to determine, among other things, such causes of illness as sorcery and breach of taboo; he could, in fact, exercise sorcery himself. The sucking doctor worked on the disease-object intrusion theory: it was his function to remove the cause of sickness by sucking it out of the patient's body. Although the tent-shaking technique was the more dramatic method employed by the conjuror together with skillful ventriloquism, showmanship was not lacking in the sucking doctor. Both were solicited with gifts of tobacco, which, if accepted, meant the doctor would undertake a cure at a specified time and for a specified fee. Each worked with an assistant who took charge of the physical arrangements and did the drumming. Each doctor accompanied his singing with a rattle. The ceremonies ordinarily were held in the evening or at night, and a small group of witnesses were present.

The *Wa'beno*, on the other hand, while also having achieved his power during the days of his early vision quest, too often used it to inflict harm. He excelled in jugglery and other tricks. He could plunge his hands into boiling water or hot syrup without the slightest discomfort, and could assume the shapes of various animals, like the bear and the fox, and sometimes he was seen at night in the guise of a fireball. Because of his knowledge of plants and their properties, he was consulted for the purpose of obtaining hunting charms and love charms, the latter for the particular purpose of entrapping the affections of someone who was reluctant to reciprocate. Skinner cites a carved wooden figure of a *Wa'beno*, nearly life size, but there seems to have been just the one figure. Hoffman suggests that the *Wa'beno*, among the Menomini at least, was as powerful as the *Mide'* priest.

The shamans exploited a variety of fetishes—objects thought to possess the magical power to induce particular effects. Generally these were wooden figurines in human form. For love magic, to attract a partner or to hold a marriage together, the shaman used a male and a female figure, bound together. Chest cavities were cut into some figures to hold certain magical items, including smaller figurines; these could be used for either such beneficent purposes as inducing good health or for the malevolent intention of causing ill health or even death. Facial paralysis was considered to be the result of such sorcery. Another fetish intended to bring about evil was a carved owl set on a pole that was stuck in the ground.

The principle of sympathetic magic—that like produces like—was exploited a great deal. By tying together a pair of puppets, the shaman transmitted the client's wish for a life situation that would bring a couple together in love. Puppets were used by a shaman for magical tricks to impress an audience with his powers. A pair of puppets were attached to sticks that, when manipulated but concealed within a yarn bag, caused the puppets to rise into public view and then disappear as if by magic. Some of the finest wood sculpture of the Woodland Indians is shown in the fetish figures.

If an individual suspected that a shaman was working evil against him, he might engage another shaman to counteract it, and thus shaman duels arose.

The conjuror used a special tent or wigwam, built according to his personal dream, but while it varied somewhat in shape and in the number and kinds of poles, it was basically a pole framework about three feet in diameter and seven feet high. The cylindrical sides were covered with skins, birch bark, or blankets to conceal the shaman; the dome-shaped top, however, was left uncovered for the entrance of those spirits that would help him. The conjuror then called on certain supernatural spirits to

Owl fetish. Chippewa.

Shaman's fetish, disassembled. Chippewa.

Shaman's fetish. Chippewa.

come into the tent. The most important of these was the turtle, which was also significant to the *Wa'beno,* for he hung the dried shell of a snapping turtle from his little tambourine drum. When the spirits entered the tent, it would shake so violently that witnesses said the top sometimes seemed to touch the ground. The conjuror consulted with these spirits, each of which had a distinctive voice and spoke in a cabalistic tongue comprehensible only to the shaman. Some of these men were reported to be skilled ventriloquists. The spirits provided the information necessary to solve such problems as the location of missing persons or lost articles, and the source of disease. They also indicated to the shaman whether or not the disease was natural or had supernatural causes: sorcery, spirit intrusion, disease-object intrusion, breach of taboo, or soul loss.

With this intelligence, then, the shaman could prescribe a cure or pass on information that would help solve the client's particular problem. It was believed that the conjuror possessed the power to call forth an individual's soul and, in this way, deprive him of reason or of life itself. He could also release the spirit from his own body and send it off to learn what caused the illness in one of his patients.

The sucking doctor operated on the theory of disease-object intrusion, and he sucked the offending foreign matter from the patient's body. After he had accepted the initial gift of tobacco that constituted a request for treatment, the doctor stipulated the time, the place, and the price of the ceremony. This, too, was usually indoors and after sundown. The group would include the doctor, his assistant or runner, the patient, and a few spectators, often friends or relatives of the patient. Dogs were banned from the vicinity as their barking might cause the doctor to choke while swallowing the tubes. The doctor's personal equipment consisted of a small tambourine drum, a gourd or tin-can rattle, and two or three tubes that were kept in a buckskin bag or cloth wrapping. The tubes, exposed only at curings, were ordinarily sections of canon bone of a deer, about three inches long and three quarters of an inch at the outer diameter. In more recent times, the tubes were brass cartridge cases with the ends removed.

After everyone was seated, the doctor took the tubes from their wrappings and placed them in a shallow dish that, according to his instructions, would hold water, maple-sugar water, salt water, or whiskey. Since each doctor obtained his personal instructions from his guardian spirit through dreams, there were many such minor variations in equipment and technique. The patient, usually partially stripped, was stretched out on the floor, a blanket under him. Tobacco was passed, and each person would take a pinch. The doctor dedicated the tobacco to the spirits; he related part of his fasting dream and enlisted the aid of one or more of his *manidog* to help. All the while, he shook his rattle and was accompanied by the assistant's drumming. It was during the song that the spirit entered the doctor's body; then, as he knelt over the patient, the

Conjurer standing near framework of conjuring wigwam. Chippewa.

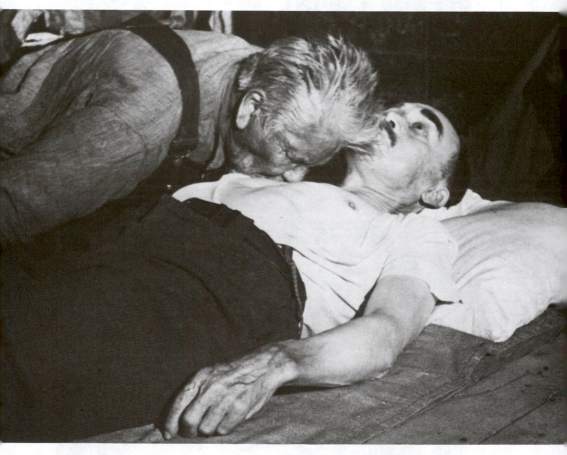

Sucking doctor at work. Chippewa.

doctor "swallowed" and regurgitated one of the tubes. With the tube projecting from his mouth he kneeled over the patient, moving about until he located the place where the sickness originated, sucked out the object through the tube, and spit both it and the tube into the shallow dish.

At this point the drumming would cease abruptly, indicating the end of that phase. The dish was passed around for inspection, and, if any foreign matter had been drawn out of the patient, the contents of the dish were thrown into the fire. Several such suckings might occur before any matter was visible in the dish. In case of complete failure, the patient would be told to return the next evening, when another spirit would be summoned. A curing ritual might last from a half hour to two hours, depending upon the success or wishes of the doctor.

Other Curative Techniques

The Woodland Indians employed three techniques of mechanical curing: cupping, tattooing, and the sweat bath.

On the whole, the cupping practitioners were women (bepe'swe-'jikwe, literally, cutting or scratching women, in Chippewa), and there were no cult or supernatural procedures connected with it. An apprentice could acquire the technique and knowledge for a fee. The patient gave the doctor a fee, tobacco, of course, plus one common article, such as a blanket. The most common ailments handled in this manner were headaches and blood poisoning. However, such maladies as dizziness, soreness, swelling, and rheumatism were also regarded as curable by this technique.

The equipment consisted of a sharp instrument for making the incision and a section of horn to draw off the blood. The cupping device was made from the small end of a cow's horn, three or four inches long, which had been cleaned out and the tip perforated. To cure a headache, for example, the doctor made a slanting incision in the patient's temple in order to strike a vein; she put the large end of the horn over the cut and then sucked on the small end to draw off the blood, which was caught in a dish; it was emptied outside in an isolated spot "where no one will step on it or disturb it." Bloodletting was limited to the head and limbs. In the case of blood poisoning, the individual was bled until "all the dark blood was out and the blood ran red and clear." A pint seemed to be about the maximum removed at any one time. No sterilization of the lancet was reported, but some doctors applied a native salve to the cut after the bleeding had stopped. A native astringent was also employed to stop the bleeding. When a metal lancet was used, the point was placed over a vein and lightly snapped with the thumb and finder to make the cut. In some cases two or three treatments, over a period of several weeks, were necessary before a cure was effected. Although bloodletting was not practiced scientifically by the Indians, it undoubtedly effected cures in some instances. That it can have a salutary physiological effect is indicated by the fact that modern medical science makes considerable use of it in cases of hypertension and erythema, a morbid redness of the skin due to congestion of the capillaries.

Whether cupping was a primitive method or one taken over from the white man is open to question. There is no archaeological evidence so far to support the theory that the Indians practiced it prehistorically. However, its exceedingly wide distribution among the historic tribes of American Indians strongly suggests a native origin.

"Tattooing" was another technique for treating the same ailments as were dealt with by cupping. The term tattooing is somewhat misleading, but it is the one to which the Indians themselves referred when speaking in English. The individual specialists, mostly women, worked without supernatural assistance, for a fee of tobacco accompanied by the usual blanket or beadwork. The patient's sore area was struck repeatedly with an instrument into which were set a series of needles. In former times the tattooing instrument was either the upper or lower jaw of a garfish; the long rows of needle-like teeth served remarkably well. The instrument was first dipped into a native medicine, then "hammered" onto the sore spot. Medicine was always applied in conjunction with tattooing, often in the form of a poultice. The purpose of the tattooing was to pierce the skin so the medicine would penetrate the blood stream; as a result, blood was frequently drawn. A Chippewa informant explained that the excruciating pain experienced during the treatment was really the soreness leaving the body. The efficacy of this method of healing, in terms of modern medical theory, can be accounted for by the idea that any such irritation attracts blood, "the great healer," to the sore area; this is somewhat akin to the theory that a mild irritation is set up by directing ultraviolet rays onto a sore or injured area. Tattooing, at the present time, is rarely practiced.

Other surgical techniques included amputation and tooth extraction. Fractured limbs were bound with basswood cords to splints made of cedar or heavy birch bark.

The chief purpose of the sweat bath was curative, although it played a prominent part in the ritual of the Mide'wiwin as well as being taken while on the hunt for the purpose of "getting rid of human odors." It was resorted to for the relief of such ailments as colds, fevers, and rheumatism.

The sweat lodge was, indeed, a small wigwam, the whole completely covered with birch bark or blankets. For the Mide'wiwin, however, it was built large enough to accommodate four men, while the one erected for curative purposes had only two poles and was just large enough for one person. When it was finished, heated stones were carried inside. The patient, who was stripped, created the steam by sprinkling water on the stones with a bunch of grass or cedar boughs. The water sometimes contained medicine or it could be used alone. In the instance we observed, cedar boughs had been steeped in the water.

According to Densmore (1928, p. 331), "after the bath the person was thoroughly rubbed, warmly wrapped and put to bed." She continues,

> Another method of steaming was used chiefly for rheumatic limbs, and with the water they put any sort of medicine which was supposed to be good for that ailment. In giving this treatment a hole was dug in the ground the size of the kettle containing the hot decoction. They put the kettle into this hole and the person sat beside it, covering his limbs closely with a blanket. A medicine frequently used in this connection was identified as willow (species doubtful). The prepared root was put in hot water and allowed to boil a short time. It was usually cooled before using.
>
> Dry herbs were also placed on heated stones and the fumes were inhaled, this treatment being used chiefly for headaches. The stones were somewhat smaller than those used in the sweat lodge, being "about the size of a small bowl." The patient covered his head and shoulders with a blanket, inclosing the stones and inhaling the fumes. A mixture of many varieties of flowers was said to be an agreeable preparation for this use.

The sweat bath was used almost universally by tribes of North America, and it extended into Middle America as far south as Guatemala. Every North American tribe had some form of it except for the Shoshone, Yuma, Pima, some of the coastal tribes of British Columbia, and the Central and Eastern Eskimo.

Preventive Measures

A variety of protective or preventive measures against illness were employed by the Woodland tribes; some were individual and some were group efforts. They did not distinguish between medicine, as we use the term, and charms; in fact, the Chippewa term for medicine, mushki'ki, included both categories. As the term is used here, however, it includes only those substances that were administered directly to an individual for either curative or malevolent purposes. Charms include substances that would affect either man or nature without material contact.

Charms, like medicine, were nearly always purchased from another individual. They were the means of assuring good fortune in hunting, fishing, trapping, gambling, war and love. They protected the Indian from disease or bodily injury. They could also be used for malevolent purposes, but the vast majority of charms were concerned with the food quest, and hunting charms were nearly as numerous. In most instances, the charm was carried in a small buckskin packet on the person. Love charms and those to be used for malicious intent were commonly worked in the home.

These charms were applied to the clothing, hair, or any personal article of the one to be affected. Songs ordinarily were not used with the charms, but rather the efficacy was secured by one's talking and praying. Protective or preventive charms included:

Flagroot, carried on the person to keep away snakes. As there are no poisonous snakes in the Woodland area, the purpose of the charm was based, apparently, either on a dislike of them or on a fear of their supernatural powers.

Dogbane, used as a protective charm against evil influence or against bad medicine.

Seneca snakeroot, used as a charm for safety on a journey.

The root of a species of milkwort, *Polygala senega L.,* carried on the person for general health and for safety on a journey.

Dream fetishes were sacred personal articles one retained throughout life, guarding him against any harm or misfortune. They were made, or obtained, according to the instructions received in one's own fasting dream. They could be acquired as the result of a dream of a close relative or namesake, wɛʲɛ, who, as we have noted, may have presented the article to him in infancy or childhood, which article was referred to by the special term *ishiu'winən.* A dream fetish may have originated as the result of intelligence received by the conjuror during his tent-shaking seance. Such objects were accorded special care and handling; they were hung on the loop of a child's cradle board and were hung, as well, over the bed of an adult. The fetish object was to be retained for life, and, if it was accidentally destroyed or worn out, it was replaced with a counterpart. These articles were taken to religious ceremonies, carried on long journeys, and, at the death of the individual, buried with him.

Tobacco offerings to the thunderbirds were a common method of securing protection against property damage and physical injury during a windstorm. When a storm came up, a piece of cut plug tobacco was placed on a stump in the yard, or a pinch of tobacco was thrown into the fire. In some cases the individual spoke to the thunderbirds, asking for protection, but this was not necessary—the offering itself was sufficient. A Chippewa informant once related, with great delight, how he camped with a party of hunters in Minnesota. A great cloud came up, and the Indians, knowing that the thunderbirds were coming, threw tobacco in the fire. The storm damaged many houses that belonged to whites, but none of the Indians' wigwams were harmed. Later some of the white people asked why, said the informant smiling; he confided that the white men didn't know about thunderbirds, that only Indians could protect themselves in this way.

Another way of preserving individual health was by faithfully observing certain taboos. In some instances the breach of taboo affected the transgressor, but more often it resulted in injury to someone else. Although the majority of taboos in Woodland culture did not concern health, in two categories, the menstrual and mourning taboos, they were not only associated with bodily injury but could be lethal.

The Indians believed that contact with a menstruating woman or anything she touched was exceedingly harmful. Kinietz (1947, p. 125) said that "those who touched her or anything she had handled such as food, water or clothing, would become very sick. She was even warned to be careful about touching herself. Formerly, menstruating girls used sticks to scratch their heads or other parts of their bodies because using a comb might cause their hair to fall out. Scratching the body might cause the finger nails to drop off or raise blisters on the skin." Girls received instructions concerning this taboo during the puberty fast at the time of their first menses. They were isolated in a special hut for a week or more, during which time they were brought food but cooked it themselves, on their own fire, and ate it in special dishes reserved for this purpose. They were warned not to bathe in the lake for fear of killing the rice crop. A menstruating woman was never to step over a young child or over a man's clothing, for sickness or even death could be the result. A young married couple was admonished not to have intercourse during the woman's catamenial period, or else the man would sicken and possibly die. It was said that, even if a menstruating woman crossed the path of a man, he could be harmed. It was also thought that if a woman was mean enough she could cripple a man by putting some menstrual blood in his food or on his clothing. One case was reported of a woman who inadvertently stepped over the cap of her son. She steamed the cap and the lad wore it, but his eye became sore; then one side of his face became paralyzed, and, finally, he died.

A person in mourning was not allowed to touch children until after the removal-of-mourning ceremony. During this period, the mourner's touch could produce sickness or even cause the death of a child. We were informed that a certain Chippewa man, paralyzed on one side, was so afflicted because a woman in mourning had picked him up, by accident, when he was small.

Among the Wisconsin Chippewa an interesting method of protecting the health of either the entire community or an individual was that of sympathetic magic employed by a group. It was thought that by obliterating a straw man especially constructed for this purpose, impending sickness could be warded off. The ceremonial pattern was simple. When, in a dream, an individual was warned by his guardian spirit that disease or illness was about to strike the community, he sent out a runner. Tobacco, as usual, was the method of invitation to these special feasts, the runner presenting each family with a bit of cut plug tobacco or Standard. He told them when and where to assemble and to bring the equipment "to make an image."

At the appointed time the people appeared with food and tobacco, the men carrying guns, the women and children with knives, clubs, and axes. The dreamer related his dream to the throng and explained why he had called them together. Food was laid out on the floor, and tobacco was passed around and smoked while the dreamer dedicated both food and tobacco to the *manidog,* asking their blessing on the proceedings. Both the food, as it was being eaten, and the tobacco, in the form of smoke, found their way to the spirits. Then the men with their guns and the women and children carrying their weapons went outdoors and cautiously approached the straw man, which had been set up by the runner a short distance from the house. The figure, made either by the runner the night before or by the women just before the ceremony began, was constructed out of straw or hay so that it would burn. It varied in height from about two to four feet and was dressed in a miniature male costume. As the crowd approached the straw man, the dreamer gave the signal for the men to shoot it, and he joined them. Then the women and children rushed up to club it, cut it, and chop it to bits. The remains were gathered up, by either the crowd or the runner, placed in a pile, and burned. The dreamer then thanked the entire assembly for their assistance.

Another instance of a group attempt to ward off impending disaster was through the technique of the "offering tree." Here, too, an individual would be warned by his guardian spirit that sickness was about to descend on the community. Invitational tobacco was carried to a number of people by the runner, who informed them where and when to assemble "to make an offering" of clothes. At the appointed time they would come, bringing food, tobacco, and articles of clothing. The food was spread out and the tobacco passed, both of them being offered to the *manidog* of the air, particularly the thunderbirds. This was done by the dreamer or by someone he had already designated to speak for him. The dreamer related his dream and told the *manidog* that this offering of clothing was in their honor, and he implored their intercession in warding off the sickness.

After the feast, the clothing and tobacco brought by the participants were hung on a tree or pole. In the ceremony observed by Robert Ritzenthaler, the clothing was tied in bunches and hung about two thirds of the way up a slender pine eighteen feet tall, from which all the branches had been trimmed except for a few at the top. In other instances a slender pine was cut, peeled, and trimmed, with just a tuft of branches left at the top. The clothing and tobacco were tied near the top, and the pole was either leaned up against the house or set upright in the ground. The clothing was supposed to be those items worn close to the body, not overcoats or other outerwear. The articles one generally saw on the pole or tree included underwear, pants, shirts, dresses, and aprons. They were to be left hanging for at least four days, and during that time they were accepted by the *manidog.* In some instances they were allowed to remain until they disintegrated. In other cases they were taken down on the fifth day and used for dishrags. Occasionally a Brave, or Chief, Dance followed the ceremony of clothes hanging.

Offering tree. Chippewa.

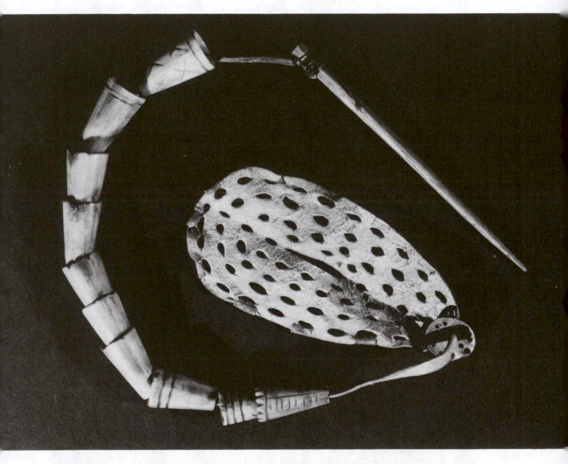

8

Games

Games, among the Woodland Indians, were played not merely for recreation but also for significant religious reasons—to honor the spirits and to cure the sick. There were games of dexterity and games of chance. Betting was also customary, for the American Indians were inveterate gamblers. In addition there were games for children, and, later, modern cards and card games were taken over from the white man. Games were played by men, by women, and by the children, but only rarely did the two sexes, as adults, play together.

Lacrosse

The most popular men's game in the Woodland area was the ball game called lacrosse. The name was derived from the French *jeu de crosse,* for the bat or racket with which the game was played. Among the Menomini it was a mimic war game believed to have been given the men by the Thunderer *manidog,* whose property it was considered to be. Among the Huron it was a curative game.

A game would be called by a man whose guardian spirit was the thunderbird, and the game was played to honor that spirit. He who called the game did not play, but stood on the sidelines offering prayers and sacrifices. He also presented the players with prizes, which were often brightly colored cloth strung on a rack to one side of the playing field. The Potawatomi gave out these prizes for each goal that was made.

The ball, about the size of a baseball, had a deerskin cover and was stuffed with hair. Formerly, a knot of wood was charred until reduced to the proper size, or a ball was cut by hand out of willow. Some tribes carved designs on the ball—stars, circles, or crosses—and others painted it a symbolic red and black, or red and yellow, which were probably the symbols of the moieties. Each man had his own racket, a sapling about three feet, ten inches long and bent at one end to form a circular loop that was filled with a leather network. The Iroquois racket had a larger, trianguloid network; when the white man took over the game from the Indian, he also appropriated this style of racket.

Among the Potawatomi, the players were invited by the regular gift of tobacco, and on the appointed day, when everyone had assembled, tobacco and food were spread on the ground and dedicated to the spirit being honored. The sponsor selected two captains. One of them was blindfolded and was led to the pile of rackets (thrown down by each man as he arrived), pulled out the sticks, and placed them in two piles. Since each racket had identifying marks on it, as each man retrieved his stick the two sides were formed. Ordinarily two teams of five each were invited, but as many as nine sometimes joined in, and old accounts of some tribes tell of as many as forty to a hundred or more on each team. There were intertribal contests, in which groups like the Sauk, Fox, and Kickapoo played moiety against moiety.

The field was a level area with two goal posts (some Chippewa groups in Minnesota used but one goal post) set in the ground about a quarter mile apart. In winter, it was sometimes played on a frozen lake. The sponsor started the game with his own racket by tossing the ball into the air in mid-field. The players either picked the ball off the ground with their rackets or caught passes from teammates. The object was to run with the ball or pass it and score a goal by hitting the post behind the opposing players or by sending the ball between the posts. One man acted as goalie. A player could not touch the ball with his hands. The opposing team attempted to intercept the ball or knock it out of a man's racket. In the melee of flying rackets, head and arm bruises, even broken limbs, were not uncommon—lacrosse was said to have been an exceedingly rough game. Generally, the fastest runners scored the most goals, but teamwork was important. A game lasted until five (for the Potawatomi) goals were scored and the five (or as many as the sponsor had decided upon) prizes had been won. A game often lasted three hours or more; some ran all day. The player who scored a goal immediately claimed his piece of yard goods, which he presented to some woman in the audience. She, in turn, would reciprocate with a gift at some future time. This exchange of gifts, among many of the Woodland groups, was a manifestation of the close ties between an uncle and his cross-niece, a young man and his cross-aunt, or vice versa.

According to Skinner (1921, p. 56) the players profited only from the sponsor's prizes, and no wagers were made. But Hoffman (1896, p. 244) indicated that when the game had degenerated from a religious rite that was played before the *Midé'wiwin* ceremonies to one played merely for amusement, personal wagers were made on the final results. The Potawatomi placed wagers at all their games, but the last game our informant remembered was played in 1946. Not many lacrosse games are played any more.

Among the Mexican Kickapoo in 1955, however, lacrosse was still significant, the opposing sides being formed from the two moieties in the village, the White and the Black. Ashes were worn by the White moiety,

Double ball and stick, and lacrosse ball and racket. Chippewa.

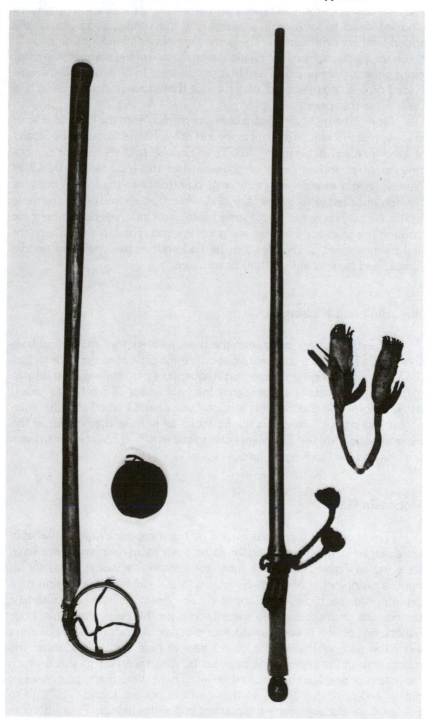

and charcoal or carbon was rubbed on members of the Black. The players stripped down to loincloths, leggings, and moccasins, and occasionally added feathers on the head. The game sometimes lasted for four days (a holdover, perhaps, from the religious significance of the number four), but more generally for one day, and four points were to be scored. Bets were placed on each point scored, with the side that scored the point collecting the bet for that point.

One of the most significant lacrosse games, from the historical point of view, was that played in front of the fort at Michilimackinac at the Straits of Mackinac, in Michigan, in 1763. To the British soldiers it was a demonstration of an Indian game of prowess, but the Indians, led by Chief Pontiac, had planned it as a ruse to gain entrance to the fort. A ball was cleverly knocked close to the gate, and, when they rushed over to retrieve it, the ballplayers were transformed into ferocious warriors swarming through the gate, and eventual slaughter ensued. The fort's commandant had been warned of the plot, but he had chosen to consider it an idle rumor, and no precautions had been taken.

Wrestling and Kicking

Wrestling was popular with the men, as were foot racing and bow shooting, all done in a competitive spirit. Among the Menomini, as well as the Winnebago, a rough game that frequently started when a crowd was gathered, and usually deteroirated into a free-for-all fight, was called Ato'wi. Someone shouted this in a loud voice, and immediately the men began kicking each other on the buttocks as hard as they could, all the while shouting Ato'wi. The object was to see who best could keep an even temper and for the longest time.

Moccasin Game

The moccasin game was played by the men, and wagers invariably were placed by those watching the game. Four men (the number seems to have varied depending on the tribe: some used five, some eight) sat on opposite sides of a blanket. Nearby was a drummer (Menomini) or a drummer for each player (Chippewa). The drummer sang and played a tambourine drum; there were special songs for this particular game. Four bullets, one of which was marked, four moccasins, and sticks for counters were the paraphernalia. The object was to hide the bullets under the moccasins, in full sight of the opponents, who then had to guess which moccasin concealed the marked bullet. There were many pretenses of hiding and removing them, so that one's opponent found it difficult to guess with accuracy where the marked bullet was hidden. Four attempts were allowed, and then the next player had a turn. The Potawatomi used just one bullet with four moccasins. The Chippewa, Winnebago, and Menomini used a "striking stick" to turn over the moccasin thought to hide the bullet. When neighboring tribes visited each other, the players were usually chosen from opposing tribes. When the government annuities were given out at Madeline Island, much of the money was redistributed by gambling on the moccasin game. Early white settlers took over the game so zealously that in Indiana a statute expressly forbade gambling at the moccasin game (among other gambling games), and stiff fines were set.

Hand Game

The hand game was another guessing game, which consisted of hiding two small objects in the hands of the players. The opponent was to guess the correct hands in which the objects were hidden, for any number could play. Fairly small articles were used—a horseshoe nail wound with string or a pebble sewn into a piece of cloth. Sharpened sticks were thrust into the ground to keep the score.

Double Ball

The double ball game, played only by the women, somewhat resembled lacrosse. The double ball was composed of two oblong buckskin bags joined together by an eight-inch buckskin thong. The Potawatomi played with just five on a side, each woman equipped with a straight stick three or four feet long. The Chippewa, however, had many more players on a side, and each one used a pair of sticks that had slight curves at the striking ends. The object was to hit the opponent's goal, the goal posts being about three hundred feet from each other. As in lacrosse, the goalies endeavored to protect their own goal. The double ball was thrown into the center of the field, and points were scored when a player finally hit the opposing goal with her two sticks (or stick) or with the double ball. This game, too, called for sturdy women and swift runners, and many a head must have been injured. The sticks had identifying marks of paint and colored ribbons. Among the Potawatomi women it was played much like lacrosse, with sponsors who called and started the game and furnished the prizes, but who did not play themselves. The men spectators yelled and whooped when a goal was scored; the woman winning a prize would give it to a spectator (very possibly her cross-uncle), who was obligated to return a gift of equal value at a later time.

Snow snake game.

"Dice" game. Winnebago.

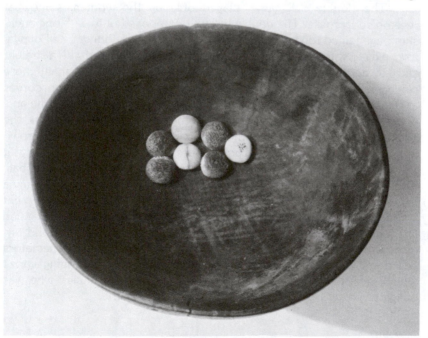

Dice

The dice game was played mostly by the women in winter, in place of double ball. This, too, was sponsored by a woman to honor her guardian spirit, and the ceremonial preliminaries were similar to those of double ball and lacrosse.

Here is a description of a Potawatomi game: After the feast, a blanket was spread out on the floor, and the women, divided into two teams, sat facing each other, each side in a semicircle. Any number of women could play, but there were only four prizes—yard goods of red, blue, green, and white. The gaming equipment consisted of a wooden bowl and eight dice; six were thin circular disks, one was carved in the form of a turtle, and one represented a horse's head. They were formerly made of buffalo rib, but horse ribs were common in later days. One surface of each die was colored blue, or sometimes red. It therefore had a colored and a white side. The bowl was held with both hands and the dice shaken to the far side of the bowl. Then the bowl was given one flip and set on the floor; then the score was counted, as follows:

All of similar color except 2	1 point
All of similar color except 1	3 points
All of similar color except turtle	5 points
All of similar color except horse	10 points
All of similar color	8 points
All of similar color except turtle and horse	10 points

The scoring, of course, would vary with each group, and Densmore simply dismissed the scoring by saying that it was "complicated." The score was tallied by the woman laying out the correct number of bean counters in front of her. Each woman shook until she missed twice; then she passed the bowl in clockwise rotation. The first one to score ten points won the game, and her prize, a piece of the yard goods, was given to one of the men spectators, who, in turn, was obliged to reciprocate with a gift of equal value in the future.

Menomini dice were made of deerhorn, plum stones, or even pieces of wood, and they, too, indicated with counters when the game was won. The Chippewa also used plum stones (they called the game, in fact, plum stones), and both men and women played. The plum stones were carved to represent various images—a fish, a hand, a man, a canoe—the object being to make the figures stand upright.

Cup and Pin

The cup and pin game was old and had several names: bone game, and ring and pin. It was played by both men and women, but Skinner

(1921, p. 369) says it was played by the Menomini only as a hunting charm. Ten dewclaws of deer were strung on a narrow piece of deer hide. At one end was an oval piece of leather with small holes, twenty-five in some cases, and at the other end was a long needle of bone or wood. When cultural changes occurred, a brass thimble replaced the bone next to the leather, and a darning needle was substituted for the bone needle.

The Chippewa manner of play was described by Densmore (1929, p. 117) as follows:

> If a considerable number are to play this game, they are divided into two sides. Each side has a leader who chooses the men who are to play on his side. Before the play begins they decide how many points shall constitute a game and how many points shall be scored by the most difficult play in the game, which is known as "catching the bone next the tail." A player continues his play as long as he scores, passing the game implement to his opponents when he fails to make a score. . . . A player holds the needle between the thumb and forefinger of his right hand; he then extends his right arm, the needle point upward, and the bones falling below his thumb. He then takes the bit of leather in his left hand and draws it backward toward his body until the string of bones is in a horizontal position. With a quick motion of his hands he releases the bit of leather, swings the string of bones forward and catches one or more of the bones on the needle, the object being to hold a series of bones in an erect position on the needle.
>
> The score is as follows: To catch the bone next the needle and hold all the bones erect on the needle counts 10: to catch any bone in the series and hold only that bone counts 1, the number in every instance corresponding to the number of bones held erect on the needle. To catch a bit of leather secures a score corresponding to the number of holes in the leather, and to catch the heavy bone or the thimble next the bit of leather counts the value decided upon before the beginning of the game. The number of points in a game is frequently 100, though any number may constitute a game. It is said that the score is "shouted by everybody," so there is no need of counters. The games are indicated by sticks placed upright in the ground.

Snow Snake

The game of snow snake was played in winter by the men and boys on the frozen lakes. It was played with a hardwood stick two to six feet long and a half to three quarters inch thick. The stick had a slightly bulbous end that resembled the head of a snake, with eyes traced on it and a crosscut to mark the mouth. The entire stick was carefully smoothed.

With his forefinger the man would hold the tapered end lightly, his thumb on one side, while he balanced it with his other hand. He took a short run, then bent and flipped the snake so it would race along the top of the ice or snow. Wagers were made on whose snake could travel the farthest. Snow snake is no longer played by the Indians of the western Great Lakes, but it is still a popular sport among the Iroquois. Their snakes were the most beautiful, due to much polishing and waxing; they were also the longest, from four to eight feet, and they were weighted with lead to gain distance. The Iroquois prepared a snow ramp, which gave additional speed at the release, and, by dragging a log through the snow, they pressed down a track that was sometimes a mile long.

Children's Games

In addition to the girls' dolls and the boys' bows and arrows, the children early learned all the games already mentioned, but in addition they had a few of their own. They played a game that was similar to cup and pin, but with a pointed stick and a bunch of grass tied to an end of a short string or cord. There was also a game made of a birchbark hoop. Mothers would encourage their youngsters to roll these hoops just before dark, so they would soon tire and sleep well. A game reminiscent of quoits consisted of a small ring fashioned from a leg bone of an animal, and a sharp metal point set in a wooden handle; it was the ring, however, that was set on the ground, and the awl that was thrown toward it, the purpose being to have the awl stand upright inside the ring.

9

Music

The music of the Woodland Indians was not purely music for the sake of music but, like their religion, it was an integral and essential element of their everyday lives. Songs accompanied ceremonies for the dead, the preparations for war, and nearly all the games; they were essential in treating the sick. For the observance of the *Mide'* rites, the songs were as indispensable as the priests themselves; there could be no ritual without music. Many songs were inspired by dreams, either an individual's dream during his vision quest or one dreamed later in his life. A song could be learned from its originator and, in some cases, it could be bought from the owner. Songs were often passed from tribe to tribe, and men returning from journeys were asked what new songs they had learned.

The instruments were few: drums, rattles, and the lovers', or courting, flutes. There were whistles made from reed, split alder, or bone, but they were not used as musical instruments. Rather, they were employed as signals during wartime, and they also played a role in the war-bundle ceremonies (Skinner, 1921, p. 355). Hoffman (1896, p. 262) describes how one was secreted in an otter medicine bag to give the impression, when blown, that the spirit of the dead animal was, indeed, inside the bag. There was the large drum for the Drum, or Dream, Dance, the water drum for the *Mide'wiwin* rites, and the tambourine drum used in the War Dance, moccasin game, and by the curing doctors and jugglers.

The water drum was fashioned from a hollowed log. It was about fifteen inches long, with one solid end; the other end was covered with a heavy piece of tanned buckskin held down with a wooden rim. Through a hole in the side, water could be poured to a depth of three or four inches and the drum shaken to wet the head or skin. It was beaten with a curved drumstick, producing on the dampened head a soft sound, but one that carried well.

The tambourine drum was a circular wooden frame about a foot and a half in diameter and two and a half inches wide. This was completely covered with thin rawhide, and ordinarily it would be painted, sometimes with the symbols of the owner's vision. Strung across the interior, near

Mnemonic boards. Menomini.

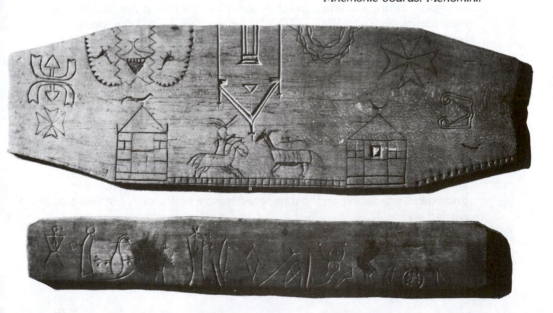

each head, were two parallel cords to which short sticks had been attached. The drummer put one hand through a rawhide loop attached to the frame; then, resting the lower side of the drum on his knee, he struck the drumhead with the wrapped end of a straight drumstick. The tambourine effect was produced by the sticks inside the drum vibrating against the heads.

The largest and most dramatically decorated drum was that which accompanied the Drum Dance (see P.84), or Dream Dance, as it was often called. The bottom of a large wooden washtub was removed and both top and bottom were covered with rawhide heads. The top head was painted symbolically, one half of it blue, the other red; through the center ran a yellow stripe representing the path of the sun. The drum hung suspended from four stakes set in the ground—the drum itself was never allowed to touch the ground—and it was so oriented that the painted sun path ran east and west, with the red half to the south. The stakes were heavily beaded, and the drum itself was ornamented with beaded belts, perforated silver coins, and bits of fur; beneath it was spread a piece of silk or of colored cotton, or a blanket. Around it sat a number of male singers beating their accompaniment with straight drumsticks wrapped at one end. Barrett (1911, p. 281) indicates that it was the beating of the drum, together with the smoke from the pipes, that carried the invocation up to the *manido*.

The rattle was simply a gourd, or a wooden sphere containing seeds, small pebbles, or shot; it was equipped with a wooden handle. It, too, was a necessary part of the equipment of both the medicine man and the *Mide'* priest.

The lover's flute or, more correctly, the flageolet, primarily was an instrument for courting and for playing a song being used as a love charm; occasionally, however, it was played to warn a village of an approaching war party. Some tribes insisted that the youths play their flutes outside the village, for it was thought that the soft, sweet, and pleasant tones were too seductive for the unmarried girls to resist. The flute was made of two sections of cedar joined to form a hollow cylinder about eighteen inches long and an inch and a quarter in diameter. When iron became available, the flute was then fashioned from a single piece of cedar that had been hollowed out by burning with a hot iron rod. A solid dam was left near the top, and a rectangular opening was cut on either side. Over this was fitted a wooden pitch control. The musician produced the tones by fingering six holes spaced about an inch apart. The flute was end-blown and was strictly a solo instrument.

The Indians placed great emphasis on the personality of the singer. To them the idea, the melody, and the rhythm of the song, were essential elements, more vital than the words. The *Mide'* songs, however, were in a separate category.

One characteristic of Chippewa singing, as it was of nearly all the Woodland groups, was a vibrato, or wavering tone, which was regarded as a sign of musical proficiency. A certain throatiness was evident in many songs. The nasal quality was usually confined to the so-called love songs. However, in the Drum Dance the women, accompanying the men's singing, produced a nasal, high-keyed humming by keeping their mouths closed and holding their noses partly shut with one hand. Rhythm, too, was as much a part of the composition as was the melody; the rhythm often expressed the idea, and within the song itself there was almost no variation, although the words could, and often did, vary. There was rhythm, of a sort, from the mere repetition of the simple phrases and words, for the singer derived some of his supernatural power from repetition. Among the Minnesota Chippewa, Densmore found three distinguishable rhythms: those of the War Dance, those of the Women's Dance, and those connected with the moccasin game.

The songs of the *Mide'* society, and there were several hundred of them, "represent the musical expression of religious ideas." Densmore (1910, pp.14-15) goes on:

The melody and the idea are the essential parts of a *Mide'* song, the words being forced into conformation with the melody. To accomplish this it was customary to add meaningless syllables either between the parts of a word or between the words; accents are misplaced and a word is sometimes accented differently in various parts of a song; the vowels are also given different sounds, or changed entirely. Any of these alterations are permissible. In addition to the meaningless syllables used to fill out the measures we find the ejaculations *he hi hi hi,* used in the songs associated with the "shooting of spirit power."

. . . it is permissible for different members of the *Mide'wiwin* holding high degrees to use slightly different words of the songs, but the idea of the song must always remain the same. The words serve as a key to this idea without fully expressing it. Sometimes only one or two words occur in a song. Their literal translation is meaningless, but to an instructed member of the *Mide'wiwin* they bear an occult significance. Many of the words used in the *Mide'* songs are unknown in the conversational Chippewa of the present time. This fact has made it difficult to secure satisfactory translations of these songs.

. . . a *Mide'* song is not considered complete unless the syllables *ho ho ho ho* are repeatedly given at the close. . . . A member of the *Mide'wiwin* usually begins his performance by drumming rapidly; then he gives the ejaculations, or speaks to the *Mide' manido* or makes some remarks concerning the song he is about to sing; after this he sings the song, the beat of the drum being continuous throughout. The drum appears to be an independent expression, as

Water drum

in a large majority of instances the metric unit of the drum is different from that of the voice.

The mnemonic device of recording symbols on birch bark was used extensively for the *Mide'* songs, for it was through these songs that the ancient tenets of the *Mide'wiwin* were handed down to each generation. A new member paid for the privilege of learning certain songs. The music and the medicine were intrinsic elements of the *Mide'wiwin;* one could hardly be used without the other.

Songs were an integral part, too, of curing the sick. The medicine doctor, who could be a member of the *Mide'wiwin* but was not always so, often sold a medicine after singing the particular song that assured its success, but, in this case, the song itself was never bought or sold. Charms, too, were accompanied by certain songs, and these could be purchased, the buyer obtaining both from the same person. Love charms, for instance, entailed securing personal items such as bits of clothing or hair from the person on whom the charm was to be worked. When worn by the one working the charm and singing the proper song for that charm, success was certain.

The Drum Dance had songs that were considered the property of its members; when a certain song was begun (everyone knew all the songs and to whom they belonged), the member who owned that song arose and began to dance. There were other songs that would assure good fortune at the start of a hunting expedition, and these were sung only by certain men. These same songs were sometimes chanted at the end of an initiation ceremony into the *Mide'* society. The words of such a song, recorded by Densmore (1910, p. 84) were as follows:

> *My war club*
> *Resounds through the sky*
> *To summon the animals to my call.*

Little symbolic drawings, the mnemonic devices by which the singers remembered the idea of the song, accompanied each one. There were also songs to assure a good harvest of maple sugar and wild rice.

Here is an example of a song that was sung before going to war, together with the narrative that accompanied the song picture, as recorded by Densmore (1910, p. 99):

Song of a Scalp Dance

The drawing shows the dancing circle, the men carrying scalps upon poles, the grave of the Chippewa, and the pole at the head of the grave.

Narrative.—This song carried us far into the past with its war parties and wild rejoicings of victory. It was sung on the return of the Chippewa from the Sioux country, with scalps. After the usual scalp dances there was held a special dance called a "round dance," because it took place around a grave. If possible, this was the grave of a person killed by the Sioux, often the grave of the person whose death had been avenged by the war. At the close of this "round dance" the poles bearing the scalps were stuck into the ground at the head of the grave, to stay there until the poles should decay and fall. The drawing of the song shows three scalps upheld during the dance, but only one placed at the head of the grave. This may be the scalp of the person who killed the buried Chippewa.

Social songs included those heard today during the Indian fairs and dances performed for the whites. The "Woman's Dance" was a part of this festivity, and it was performed as much for pleasure as for the exchange of gifts, which often was a part of the action. Each woman brought a few gifts, which she laid beside her. As a particular song was started, three young men, making the swooping movements associated with the Chippewa type of dancing, would dance before three young women and lay down their own gifts. In most instances the exchange of gifts was arranged beforehand. The couples danced in an ever-widening circle facing the drum, the women moving in a sidewise shuffling step, the men generally performing the high leaps and steps of the War Dance. The gifts would consist of pipes, bells, pieces of beaded clothing, pieces of calico, and occasionally a pony. Densmore described how she had seen a man on such an occasion "dance away" his beaded velvet costume, one piece at a time, finally leaving the circle with nothing to cover him but a blanket.

10

Folklore

The myths and folk tales of the Woodland groups had many characteristics in common. All tribes told of a culture hero who played the dual role of trickster or fool as well as bringer of good. As might be expected from a people living in a forest ecology, animals engaged a good deal of their attention, and this was reflected in the folklore, much of which bestowed magical powers on these creatures. The myths recounted not only the origin of the people, their clans, and the world, but also were a means of emphasizing religious values, ethical attitudes, and educational patterns. During the long winter nights they served as entertainment for both children and adults. Relating the creation myth was an intrinsic part of the *Mide'wiwin* rite; by the very power believed to be released through its telling, the story helped to heal, cure, to prolong life, and to ward off evil.

The stories of the culture hero whose grandmother was the earth formed a major portion of the folklore; these stories admonished one to "live the right kind of life" (Jones, 1919; p. 552), but when they related the foolish pranks as well as the obscenities of *Wenebojo* (the Chippewa name) he was often made to look sheepish in the end, the moral being that a good Indian did not behave in an unacceptable manner. It was *Wenebojo* who taught the Indians agriculture, hunting, the knowledge and use of medicinal plants, and the religious rites of the *Mide'wiwin;* he who brought them tobacco, saved them from storms, and, as often as not, played tricks on them. He had no compunction about killing either Indians or animals if by so doing he furthered his own ends, but by prodigious feats of magic he could bring them back to life. Sometimes *Wenebojo* was described as a rather foolish fellow; indeed, the name for him in Ottawa, *Manabush,* meant just that, though the same name in Menomini meant "great rabbit," referring to the mighty deeds he performed. Woodland humor is perhaps at its acme in the *Wenebojo* stories, and the humorous passages never failed to provoke laughter among the listeners, although they had heard them time and again. There were many relaxed and ribald references to the feces, the buttocks, the anus, and other parts of the body. There can be no doubt, however, that the Indians identified with *Wenebojo* precisely because he exhibited human characteristics and failings.

Other tales related instances of physical prowess; some accounted for natural phenomena. Stories concerning cannibalism were not uncommon, and they could have had their origin in fact; fear of starvation was ever present among these people who had to work so hard for their food. The *windigo,* important among the Forest tribes, was an ice monster who came in the winter to devour the Indians, but who was often thwarted in his attempts by a little girl and her dog, and in some cases, a kettle of boiling tallow, which when poured over the *windigo,* reduced him to a tiny core and made him vulnerable to assault. Other stories mentioned giants as well as dwarfs, and there was often someone, an Indian, one of the animals, or the culture hero himself, who possessed the magical power to make himself smaller or larger, or to bring himself back to life after being killed.

The water monster was another significant supernatural being who could invoke terror and whose machinations were incorporated in the folklore of all the Woodland tribes. Among the Winnebago it was a panther with a copper tail; among the Chippewa it was a panther or a lynx; among the Saulteaux, or Canadian Chippewa, it was the Horned Water Snake. The Menomini merely called it a great fish, but they told how it devoured many of the first people before finally being destroyed by the culture hero. In whatever form, luckily, the water monster was terrified of thunder, the noise made by the Thunderers or thunderbirds when they were protecting the Indian. Therefore, before starting out in a canoe, one must always throw offerings of tobacco on the water to propitiate the water monster and insure one's safety during the journey. Skinner (1911, p. 92) tells how an Indian boy begged a water monster to carry him across a lake, promising to warn the creature of thunder but secretly determining not to do so for fear of being carried under the surface and being drowned. When the monster heard thunder he asked the boy about it, but not until they were within easy reach of land did the boy admit hearing a clap of thunder. Whereupon the water monster, tossing his human burden aside, dove beneath the water and, at least in that particular story, worked no more evil.

Stories told in a social situation were narrated, generally, in the winter. The Chippewa said that since snakes and frogs were considered to be evil creatures, they were not permitted to listen to stories, and so the tales were related only when they were hibernating—that is, in the winter. All requests for stories were accompanied by a gift of tobacco. The Winnebago carried this even further: the person qualified to relate the origin myths of his clan refused to tell them until he had received the requisite amount of gifts. Often these included a horse, clothing, food, beads, and blankets. Then, later, at a feast, he would announce that this young Winnebago was now empowered to tell his clan's origin in the future, but that he must be approached in the proper way and with the proper gifts. It was the duty of every Winnebago to try to learn the origin of his clan.

A good storyteller was esteemed for his excellence as a dramatic entertainer, and his reputation would travel far. The myths were long, often taking many hours to relate, and were replete with repititious phrases that were well known to the listeners. However, Skinner (1911, p. 81) said that the Sauk and Fox preferred short, succinct tales. It was not unusual for a story to come to an abrupt halt, rather than to a finished ending, occasionally by the use of a phrase like "That is as far as the story goes" or "That is the way they tell it." In many cases, more than one incident was related in one story. The tales were peopled by anthropomorphic animals, birds, and fish, creatures that became the totems of various clans, and by their elder brother, who was the universal culture hero. His younger brother was nearly always a wolf, the *Chibia'bos* of the Potawatomi, the spirit who guided the souls of the dead on the four-day journey. The bear played an extremely significant role in *Mide'wiwin* myths. The otter, muskrat, skunk, ermine, beaver, loon, hell-diver, heron, Canada jay, sturgeon, crawfish, catfish—all of these, through their mythic behavior, were well known to the Woodland Indians.

The first two stories that follow were often, but not always, told together. As the prelude to the Creation myth, the story of *Wenebojo* and the Wolves is almost essential; there were variations in detail from tribe to tribe, but the same ideas were reflected in nearly all the stories.

Wenebojo and the Wolves (Wisconsin Chippewa)

One day Wenebojo saw some people and went up to see who they were. He was surprised to find that they were a pack of wolves. He called them nephews and asked what they were doing. They were hunting, said the Old Wolf, and looking for a place to camp. So they all camped together on the edge of a lake.

Wenebojo was very cold for there were only two logs for the fire, so one of the wolves jumped over the fire and immediately it burned higher. Wenebojo was hungry, so one of the wolves pulled off his moccasin and tossed it to Wenebojo and told him to pull out the sock. Wenebojo threw it back, saying that he didn't eat any stinking socks. The wolf said:

"You must be very particular if you don't like this food."

He reached into the sock and pulled out a deer tenderloin, then reached in again and brought out some bear fat. Wenebojo's eyes popped. He asked for some of the meat and started to roast it over the fire. Then, imitating the wolf, Wenebojo pulled off his moccasin and threw it at the wolf, saying, "Here, nephew, you must be hungry. Pull my sock out." But there was no sock, only old dry hay that he used to keep his feet warm. The wolf said he didn't eat hay and Wenebojo was ashamed.

The next day the wolves left to go hunting, but one, the father of the young wolves, came along with Wenebojo. As they traveled along, they found an old deer carcass. Old Wolf told Wenebojo to pick it up, but Wenebojo said he didn't want it and kicked it aside. The Wolf picked it up and shook it: it was a nice, tanned deerskin which Wenebojo wanted, so Old Wolf gave it to him. They went on, following the wolves. Wenebojo saw blood and soon they came on the pack, all lying asleep with their bellies full; only the bones were left. Wenebojo was mad because they were so greedy. The Old Wolf then woke up the others and told them to pack the deer home. Wenebojo picked up the best bones so he could boil them. When they reached camp, the fire was still burning and Old Wolf told the others to give Wenebojo some meat to cook. One of the wolves came toward Wenebojo belching and looking like he was going to throw up. Another acted the same way and suddenly, out of the mouth of one came a ham and some ribs out of the mouth of another. It is said that wolves have a double stomach, and in this way, then, can carry meat home, unspoiled, to their pups.

After that Wenebojo didn't have to leave the camp, for the wolves hunted for him and kept him supplied with deer, elk and moose. Wenebojo would prepare the meat and was well off, indeed. Toward spring the Old Wolf said they would be leaving, that Wenebojo had enough meat to last until summer. One younger wolf said he thought Wenebojo would be lonesome, so he, the best hunter, would stay with him. (This was the same Chibia'bos of the Potawatomi who guided the souls to the Land of the Dead. Some tribes called him the Nephew and some the Younger Brother of Wenebojo.)

All went well until suddenly the evil manidog became jealous of Wenebojo and decided they would take his younger brother away. That night Wenebojo dreamed his brother, while hunting a moose, would meet with misfortune. In the morning, he warned the brother not to cross a lake or stream, even a dry stream bed, without laying a stick across it. When Wolf did not return, Wenebojo feared the worst and set out to search for him. At last he came to a stream which was rapidly becoming a large river and he saw tracks of a moose and a wolf. Wenebojo realized that Wolf had been careless and neglected to place a stick across the stream.

Desolate, Wenebojo returned to his wigwam. He wanted to find out how his brother had died, so he started out to find him. He came to a big tree leaning over a stream that emptied into a lake; a bird was sitting in the tree looking down into the water. Wenebojo asked him what he was looking at. The bird said the evil manidog were going to kill Wenebojo's brother and he was waiting for some of the guts to come floating down the stream so he could eat them.

This angered Wenebojo but he slyly told the bird he would paint it if it told him what it knew. The bird said the manido, who was the chief of the water monster (or lynxes) lived on a big island up the stream, but that he and all the others came out to sun themselves on a warm day. So Wenebojo pretended he would paint the bird, but he really wanted to wring its neck. However, the bird ducked and Wenebojo only hit him on the back of the head, ruffling his feathers. This was the Kingfisher and that was how he got his ruffled crest. From now on, Wenebojo told him, the only way he would get his food would be to sit in a tree all day and wait for it.

Then Wenebojo heard a voice speaking to him. It told him to use the claw of the kingfisher for his arrow and, when he was ready to shoot the water monster, not to shoot at the body, but to look for the place where the shadow was and shoot him there. (The shadow and the soul were associated together as being the same thing. The soul of a person was his life; hence, to kill the soul was to kill life.)

Wenebojo then traveled up the stream until he came to the island where the chief of the water monsters was lying in the sun. He shot into the side of the shadow. The manido arose and began to pursue Wenebojo who ran with all his might, looking for a mountain. He was also pursued by the water, which kept coming higher and higher. At last, he found a tall pine, high up on a mountain and climbed it. Still the water continued to rise half way up the tree.

That story, having explained Wenebojo's trouble with the evil manidog resulting from his search for his wolf brother, either ended there or might continue with the Creation of the World.

Creation of the World (Wisconsin Chippewa)

Wenebojo, having outwitted the evil manidog by trickery, at last found himself stranded in the pine tree. He crept higher, begging the tree to stretch as tall as it could. Finally the waters stopped just below Wenebojo's nose. He saw a lot of animals swimming around and asked them all, in turn, to dive down and bring up a little earth, so that he and they might live. The loon tried, then the otter and the beaver, but all of them were drowned before they could bring back any earth. Finally, the muskrat went down, but he too passed out as he came to the surface.

"Poor little fellow," said Wenebojo, "You tried hard." But he saw the muskrat clutching something in his paw, a few grains of sand and a bit of mud. Wenebojo breathed on the muskrat and restored his life, then he took the mud and rolled it in his hands. Soon he had enough for a small island and he called the other *animals to climb out of the water. He sent a huge bird to fly around the island and enlarge it. The bird was gone four days (the magic number), but Wenebojo said that was not enough and he sent out the eagle to make the land larger.*

"Here," said Wenebojo, "is where my aunts and uncles and all my relatives will make their home."

Then Wenebojo cut up the body of one of the evil manidog and fed part of it to the woodchuck, who had once saved his life. Into a hollow he put the rest of the food and some of it turned into oil or fat; Wenebojo told the animals to help themselves. The woodchuck was told to work only in the summertime; in the winter he could rest in a snug den and sleep, and each spring he would have a new coat. Before that, most of the animals had lived on grass, but now they could have meat if they wished. The rabbit came and took a little stick with which he touched himself high on the back. The deer and other animals that eat grass, all touched themselves on their flanks. Wenebojo told the deer he could eat moss. The bear drank some of the fat, as did the smaller animals who eat meat. All those who sipped the fat were turned into manidog and are the guardian spirits of every Indian who fasts. Wenebojo then named the plants, herbs and roots; he instructed the Indians in the use of these plants. Wenebojo's grandmother, Nokomis, also has a lodge somewhere in that land.

How the Indians Got Maple Sugar (Chippewa and Menomini)

One day Wenebojo was standing under a maple tree. Suddenly it began to rain maple syrup—not sap—right on top of him. Wenebojo got a birchbark tray and held it out to catch the syrup. He said to himself: "This is too easy for the Indians." So he threw the syrup away and decided that before they could have the syrup, the Indians would have to give a feast, offer tobacco, speak to the manido and put out some birchbark trays.

The Menomini say that Nokomis, the grandmother of Manabush, showed him how to insert a small piece of wood into each maple tree so the sap could run down into the vessels beneath. When Manabush tested it, it was thick and sweet. He told his grandmother it would never do to give the Indians the syrup without making them work for it. He climbed to the top of one of the maples, scattered rain over all the trees, dissolving the sugar as it flowed into the birchbark vessels. Now the Indians have to cut wood, make vessels, collect the sap and boil it for a long time. This keeps them from being idle for too long a time.

How the Women Were Given Menstruation (Menomini)

Manabush was jealous of the attentions the Bear showed to Nokomis, his grandmother. One day, in a rage, he killed the Bear and went away. When he returned he noticed his grandmother had combed her hair and put on clean clothes. He suspected that someone had been there, but she made no reply which satisfied him. He went into the woods on the following day and again, when he returned, his grandmother had combed her hair and put on clean clothes. This went on for several days. Manabush suspected that it was the Bear who was visiting his grandmother, so he waited near the wigwam, very quietly. Soon, he heard the Bear coming along the trail, snorting and grunting. He made straight for the wigwam and entered it.

Manabush was furious. He got a piece of dry birchbark and lit it. With the torch in his hand, he crept up to the door of the wigwam, pulled the cover aside and saw the Bear with his grandmother. He threw the torch at the Bear and struck him on the back, just above the groin. Frantic with pain, the Bear rushed out, through the woods and down the hill to the stream. But the flames kept burning him, and finally he dropped dead. When Manabush came up to the dead body, he carried the carcass back to his grandmother's wigwam and said: "Here, grandmother, I have killed a bear; now we can have something to eat."

His grandmother asked him how he killed the Bear, but he just mumbled something, not wanting her to know how the Bear had been killed.

Then Manabush cut up the Bear and offered a piece to his grandmother, but she refused, saying: "No, my grandson, I cannot eat this. He was my husband." Angry, Manabush caught up a clot of the Bear's blood and threw it at Nokomis, hitting her in the abdomen. She replied: "For that act your aunts will always have trouble every moon, and will give birth to just such clots as this."

And that is why Indian women menstruate every month.

How the Indians Got Tobacco (Menomini)

Tobacco was given to the Indians by Manabush, who stole it from a mountain giant. Manabush had smelled the delightful odor and asked the giant to give him some. The giant informed him the spirits had been there smoking, during their annual ceremony, and he spied some bags filled with tobacco and, snatching up one of them, he ran off to the mountain tops. He was so closely pursued by the giant that only by trickery did he succeed in throwing the giant down to the ground saying, "Because you are so mean, you shall be known as the Jumper—the grasshopper. By your stained mouth everyone will know you and you will be the scourge of those who raise tobacco."

Then Manabush divided the tobacco among his brothers and in this way it came to the Indians. The grasshopper still shoots tobacco juice from its mouth.

Wenebojo and the Dancing Geese (Canadian Chippewa)

Wenebojo often took long journeys. On one of these, he happened to hear singing out on a lake, and when he looked to see who was singing, he thought he saw some people dancing. He went toward them, saying how much he would like to join them. Suddenly, he heard some loud laughter and when he looked closer, he realized that what he had thought were dancers, were really the reeds swaying in the breeze. He realized that the evil manidog had played a trick on him and he was furious.

He went on along the lake and began to get hungry. He saw some geese (or ducks) swimming a little off shore and thought to himself, "Now, I would like some of those geese to eat."

Wenebojo then gathered some balsam boughs in an old dirty blanket he was carrying and, with this on his shoulder, he called to the goslings and offered to teach them some of the songs he was carrying in his bag. They all crowded in to shore, and he told them they must dance just like he did, singing the song he would teach them.

"A dance on one leg. O my little brothers!"

And as they danced on one leg, they stretched their necks upward. Then Wenebojo sang,

"A dance with my eyes closed, O my little brothers!"

And Wenebojo danced and stretched, and the little goslings all did as he did, closing their eyes and stretching themselves. Wenebojo then moved among the foolish goslings and began to break their necks. Just then, the Loon, who had been dancing with the other birds, opened his eyes and immediately began to cry:

"Look out, we are being killed by Wenebojo!"

By this time, Wenebojo had killed several goslings, but he was so angry with the Loon that he kicked him on the small of the back. That is why the Loon has that peculiar curve to his back.

Wenebojo decided to cook his goslings there on the shore of the lake, so he buried them in the sand, putting their legs up so he could find them when they were cooked. Then he built a fire over them and lay down to sleep. He told his buttocks to keep watch for *him and, if anyone came, to wake him, for he did not want his goslings stolen.*

While Wenebojo slept some people came around a bend in the lake. They saw the goslings legs sticking up in the air and thought that Wenebojo had something good to eat. But they saw Wenebojo stir when his buttocks called him and they ducked behind some bushes to hide. Wenebojo did not see anything and scolded his buttocks for waking him unnecessarily. Again the people came out and again the buttocks woke Wenebojo, but since Wenebojo did not see them, he scolded the buttocks once more. The third time the people crept up silently, took the goslings and put the legs back just as they had found them. The buttocks remained silent because they had received only a scolding the first two times.

When Wenebojo awoke, he started to take out his goslings for he was very hungry. But he could find nothing buried in the ashes and then he was furious with his buttocks; he decided to punish them by standing over the fire until they were scorched. At last, when the buttocks were black and crisp, Wenebojo tried to walk away, but it was so painful that he could scarcely move. So he sat on the top of a steep cliff and slid down, and the sore skin of his buttocks became the lichen. As he walked along, he dragged his bleeding buttocks behind him through some dense shrubs. When he looked back, the shrubs were red from his blood. This, said Wenebojo, will be what the people will use to mix their tobacco—the red willows.

The *windigo* stories were very popular, and, it was believed, the frightening creature that stalked the winter woods could be an Indian in disguise. Any stranger who came to the village was closely watched for fear he might be a *windigo*. The children even made a game out of all this, one acting as the ice monster disguised with leaves on his head, the others searching out his hiding place. The leader would fight the child *windigo*, the other children screaming and clinging to each other, and, when the *windigo* seized one of them and pretended to eat him, their self-induced terror knew no bounds.

Here are two *windigo* stories (from the Wisconsin Chippewa), both replete with the fears and terrors of these legendary creatures. In one, the people are saved by the spirits, but in the other by a manifestation of themselves, a little girl who possessed the power to overcome evil.

Windigo

One winter a newly married couple went hunting with the other people and when they moved to the hunting grounds a child was born to them. One day, as they were fondling him in his cradle board and talking to him, the child spoke to them. They were very surprised for he was too young to talk.

"Where is that manidog̈isik (Sky Spirit)?" asked the baby. "They say he is very powerful and some day I am going to visit him."

His mother grabbed him and said, "You should not talk about that manido that way."

A few nights later, they fell asleep again with the baby in his cradle board between them. In the middle of the night the mother awoke and discovered that her baby was gone. She woke her husband and he got up, started a fire and looked all over the wigwam for the baby. They searched the neighbor's wigwam but could not find it. They lit birchbark torches and searched the community looking for tracks. At last they found some tiny tracks leading down to the lake. Halfway down to the lake they found the cradle board and they knew then the baby himself had made the tracks, had crawled out of his cradle board and was headed for the manido. The tracks leading from the cradle down to the lake were large, a cubit in length, and the parents realized that their child had turned into a windigo, the terrible ice monster who could eat people. They could see his tracks where he had walked across the lake.

The manidog̈isik had fifty smaller manidog or dwarfs to protect him. When one of these dwarfs threw a rock, it was a bolt of lightning. As the windigo approached, the dwarfs heard him coming, ran out to meet him and began to fight; finally they knocked him down with a bolt of lightning. The windigo fell dead with a noise like a big tree falling. As he lay there he looked like a big Indian, but when the people started to chop him up, he was a huge block of ice. They melted down the pieces and found, in the middle of the body, a tiny infant about six inches long with a hole in his head where the dwarf had hit him. This was the baby who had turned into a windigo. If the dwarfs had not killed it, the windigo would have eaten up the whole village.

Another common windigo story described how a girl and her dog defeated the cannibalistic monster and saved her village:

The villagers realized a windigo was coming when they saw a kettle swinging back and forth over the fire. No one was brave enough or strong enough to challenge this ice creature. After they had sent for a wise old grandmother who lived at the edge of the village, the little grandchild, hearing the old woman say she was without power to do anything, asked what was wrong. While the people moaned that they would all die, the little girl asked for two sticks of peeled sumac as long as her arms; these she took home *with her while the frightened villagers huddled together.*

That night it turned bitter cold. The child told her grandmother to melt a kettle of tallow over the fire. As the people watched, trees began to crack open and the river froze solid. All this was caused by the windigo, as tall as a white pine tree, coming over the hill.

With a sumac stick gripped in each hand, the little girl ran out to meet him. She had two dogs which ran ahead of her and killed the windigo's dog. But still the windigo came on. The little girl got bigger and bigger until, when they met, she was as big as the windigo himself. With one sumac stick, she knocked him down and with the other she crushed his skull—the sticks had turned to copper. Then, after she killed the windigo, the little girl swallowed the hot tallow and gradually grew smaller until she was herself again.

Everyone rushed over to the windigo and began to chop him up. He was made of ice, but in the center they found the body of a man with his skull crushed in. The people were very thankful and gave the little girl everything she wanted.

Here are two of the stories told in social situations that accounted for natural phenomena.

The Moon (Menomini)

Once, the Sun and his sister, the Moon, lived together in a wigwam in the east. The Sun dressed himself to go hunting and took his bow and arrows and left. He was absent such a long time that when his sister came out into the sky to look for her brother, she became alarmed. She traveled twenty days looking for the Sun; finally he returned, bringing with him a bear which he had shot.

The Sun's sister still comes up into the sky and travels for twenty days; then she dies, and for four days nothing is seen of her. At the end of that time, however, she returns to life and travels twenty days more.

The Catfish (Menomini)

Once when the Catfish were assembled in the water, an old chief said to them, "I have often seen a moose come to the edge of the water to eat grass; let us watch for him and kill and eat him. He always comes when the sun is a little way up in the sky."

The Catfish who heard this agreed to go and attack the moose. They were scattered everywhere among the grass and rushes, when the moose came slowly along picking grass. He waded down into the water, where he began to feast. The Catfish all watched to see what their old chief would do, and presently one of them worked his way slowly through the grass to where the moose's leg was, when he thrust his spear into it. Then the moose said, "What is it that has thrust a spear into my leg?"

Looking down he saw the Catfish; he immediately began to trample upon them with his hoofs, killing a great number of them, while those that escaped swam down the river as fast as they could. The Catfish still carry spears, but their heads have never recovered from the flattening they received when they were trampled into the mud by the moose.

Phonetic Key

ə as the "u" in but   č as the "ch" in child

ε as the "e" in wet   ' a glottal stop

Glossary

Algonkian The language family of the Woodland tribes.

Algonkin A Woodland tribe.

Chibia'bos (chee-bee-AH-bush) Potawatomi name for the younger brother of *Wi'ske* (Potawatomi), the Woodland culture hero. He was generally depicted as a wolf.

Coiled A basketry technique in which coils of elements are first wrapped, then sewn one on another.

Crooked Knife A steel blade with upturned end, usually made from a file. Derived from the farrier's knife.

Ishiuˀwinən (i-she-U-wi-nun) Special articles given a Chippewa child when named by his namesake and kept for the rest of his life.

Kinnikinnick Algonkian word meaning "to mix." Scrapings from the inner bark of certain willows, dried and mixed with tobacco and smoked in pipes.

Makuk (mah-KUK) Birchbark container, not waterproof, used to carry and store food.

Manabush (Mah-nah-BUSH) Also *Nanabush*. Menomini name for the Woodland culture hero.

Manido, pl. *Manidog* (Mah-nee-DOE, Mah-nee-DUG) Supernatural beings, both good and evil.

Mide' (me-DAY) Used as an adjective or noun, mystic.

139

Mide'wiwin (me-DAY-wi-win) Literally "mystic doings"; the religious curing society and its ritual.

Mi'gis (MEE-gis) Small shell or shells used in the Medicine Dance; they carry "mystic power" for good or evil.

Moiety (MOI-eh-tee) Two basic complementary tribal subdivisions. A dual division.

Muski'ki (moosh-KEE-kee) Chippewa term for medicine.

Ojibwa The Canadian term for Chippewa.

Peyote (Pay-OHT- or pay-OH-tee) A religious ceremony, incorporating Christian and Indian elements, based on eating peyote, a spineless cactus.

Runner A man assigned to carry out various mundane tasks in religious ceremonies.

Shaman (SHAY-man) A medicine man who uses supernatural powers for good or evil.

Tumpline A carrying strap with the line worn across the forehead, the burden lying across the wearer's back and shoulders.

Twined A weaving technique in which a pair of strands are passed front and back over a warp strand, giving a twisted effect.

Wabeno (WAH-be-no) Literally "morning star man" in Menomini. A shaman whose intent is generally evil.

Warp and Weft The warp is the foundation strands over which the weft threads are woven.

Wε'ε (WEH-eh—nasalized) Chippewa for both the namesake and the one who bestows the name.

Wenebojo (Way-na-BOW-zho) Chippewa name for the Woodland culture hero.

Wi'ske (WI-skay—first syllable nasalized) Potawatomi name for the Woodland culture hero.

Windigo (WIN-dih-go) Mythical cannibalistic monster, made of ice.

140

Bibliography

Barrett, S.A.
   1911. "The Dream Dance of the Chippewa and Menomini Indians of Northern Wisconsin," Bulletin of the Milwaukee Public Museum, Vol. 1 (251-406), Milwaukee.

Byers, Douglas S.
   1946. "The Environment of the Northeast." In *Man in Northeastern North America,* ed. F. Johnson. Papers of the Robert S. Peabody Foundation of Archaeology, Vol. 3, Andover, Mass.

Callender, Charles
   1962. *Social Organization of the Central Algonkian Indians.* Milwaukee Public Museum Publications in Anthropology, No. 7, Milwaukee.

Clements, Forrest E.
   1932. *Primitive Concepts of Disease.* University of California. A. & E., Vol. 32 (185-252).

Culin, Stewart
   1907. "Games of the North American Indian," Bureau of American Ethnology, Annual Report 24 (267-346), Washington, D.C.

Densmore, Frances
   1910. "Chippewa Music," Bureau of American Ethnology, Bulletin 45 (1-209), Washington, D.C.
   1913. "Chippewa Music," Bureau of American Ethnology Bulletin 53 (1-334), Washington, D.C.
   1927. "Uses of Plants by the Chippewa Indians," Bureau of American Ethnology, Annual Report 44 (275-397), Washington, D.C.
   1929. "Chippewa Customs," Bureau of American Ethnology, Bulletin 86 (1-204), Washington, D.C.
   1941. "The Study of Indian Music," Annual Report of the Smithsonian Institution (527-50), Washington, D.C.

Eggan, Fred (ed.)
   1955. "Social Anthropology: Methods and Results." In *Social Anthropology of North American Tribes,* Second Edition. University of Chicago Press.

Farb, Peter
   1963. *Ecology.* Life Nature Library, Time, Inc., New York.

Hallowell, A. Irving
1942. *The Role of Conjuring in Saulteaux Society.* University of Pennsylvania Press, Philadelphia.

Hilger, Sister M. Inez
1951. "Chippewa Child Life and Its Cultural Background," Bureau of American Ethnology, Bulletin 146. Washington, D.C.

Hoffman, Walter James
1886. "The Midewiwin or Grand Medicine Society of the Ojibwa," Bureau of American Ethnology, Annual Report 7 (143-300), Washington, D.C.
1896. "The Menomini Indians," Bureau of American Ethnology, Annual Report 14 (11-335), Washington, D.C.

Howells, W. W.
1946. "Physical Types of the Northeast," in *Man in Northeastern North America.* Frederick Johnson, ed., Papers of the R.S. Peabody Foundation of Archaeology, Andover, Mass.

Jenness, Diamond
1935. "The Ojibway Indians of Parry Island, Their Social and Religious Life," National Museum of Canada, Bulletin 78, Ottawa.

Joffe, Natalie
1940. "The Fox of Iowa," in *Acculturation in Seven American Indian Tribes.* R. Linton, ed., New York.

Johnson, Frederick (ed.)
1946. *Man in Northeastern North America.* Papers of the Robert S. Peabody Foundation for Archaeology, Vol. 3, Andover, Mass.

Jones, William
1913. "Kickapoo Ethnological Notes," American Anthropologist, 15:332-35.
1915. *Kickapoo Tales.* Publications of the American Ethnological Society, Vol. 9, New York.
1917. *Ojibwa Texts,* ed. T. Michelson. Publications of the American Ethnological Society, Vol. 7, Part 1, New York.
1919. *Ojibwa Texts,* ed. T. Michelson. Publications of the American Ethnological Society, Vol. 7, Part 2, New York.
1939. *Ethnography of the Fox Indians,* ed. Margaret W. Fisher. Bureau of American Ethnology, Bulletin 125. Washington, D.C.

Keesing, Felix M.
  1939. *The Menomini Indians of Wisconsin.* American Philosophical
  Society Memoir 10, Philadelphia.

Kinietz, W. Vernon
  1940. *The Indian Tribes of the Western Great Lakes.* Occ. Contributions No. 10, Museum of Anthropology, University of Michigan, Ann Arbor.

Kohl, J.C.
  1860. *Kitchi-Gami.* Chapman and Hall, London.

Kroeber, A.L.
  1939. *Cultural and Natural Areas of Native North America.* University of California Press, Berkeley.

Landes, Ruth
  1937. *Ojibwa Sociology.* Columbia University Contributions to
  Anthropology, Vol. 29. Columbia University Press, New York.
  1938. *The Ojibwa Woman.* Columbia University Contributions to
  Anthropology, Vol. 31. Columbia University Press, New York.
  1968. *Ojibwa Religion and the Midewiwin* University of Wisconsin
  Press, Madison.

Lawson, P.B.
  1920. "The Potawatomi," Wisconsin Archaeologist 19:41-116.

Lurie, Nancy Oestreich (ed.)
  1961. *Mountain Wolf Woman, The Autobiography of a Winnebago
  Indian.* University of Michigan Press, Ann Arbor.

Lyford, Carrie A.
  1943. *Ojibwa Crafts.* U.S. Department of the Interior Handcraft
  Series, Vol. 3, Washington, D.C.

Marriott, Alice
  1958. "Ribbon Applique' Work of North American Indians, Part I,"
  Bulletin of Oklahoma Anthropological Society Vol. VI (March)
  (49-59).

Michelson, Truman
  1927. *Contributions to Fox Ethnology.* Bureau of American Ethnology, Bulletin 85. Washington, D.C.

Mooney, James
  1928. *The Aboriginal Population of America North of Mexico.*
  Smithsonian Miscellaneous Collections, Vol. 80, No. 7, Washington, D.C.

Radin, Paul
1916. "The Winnebago Tribe," Bureau of American Ethnology, Annual Report 37 (35-560), Washington, D.C.
1920. *The Autobiography of a Winnebago Indian.* California Publications in American Archaeology and Ethnology, Vol. 16, No. 7.

Ritzenthaler, Robert E.
1953. *The Potawatomi Indians of Wisconsin.* Milwaukee Public Museum Bulletin, Vol. 19, No. 3, Milwaukee.
1954. *Chippewa Preoccupation with Health.* Milwaukee Public Museum Bulletin, Vol. 19, No. 4, Milwaukee.

Ritzenthaler, Robert E. and Peterson, F.A.
1956. *The Mexican Kickapoo.* Milwaukee Public Museum Publications in Anthropology, No. 2, Milwaukee.

Rogers, Edward S.
1962. *The Round Lake Ojibwa.* Royal Ontario Museum Paper No. 5, University of Toronto, Toronto.

Salzer, Robert
1961. "Central Algonkin Beadwork," American Indian Tradition, Vol. 7, No. 5 (166-78), Alton, Illinois.

Skinner, Alanson
1911. "Notes on the Eastern Cree and Northern Saulteaux," Anthropological Papers of the American Museum of Natural History, Vol. 9, Part 1 (1-179), New York.
1921. *Material Culture of the Menomini.* Museum of the American Indian, Heye Foundation, Notes and Monographs No. 20, New York.

Speck, F.G.
1914. "The Family Hunting Band as the Basis of Algonkian Social Organization," American Anthropologist 17:289-305.

Warren, W.W.
1885. "History of the Ojibways," Contributions of the Minnesota Historical Society, No. 5 (21-394).

Index

Butterfly design, 30
Butternuts, 21

Calumet (peace) pipe, 89, 93
Canadian tribes (see also specific tribes by name); Canadian (subarctic) Algonkians, 13-14; population, 13; physical types, 15
Cannibalism, stories of, 128, 135-36
Canoes, 11, 12, 51, 62, 65
Caribou, 15
Catfish, folklore of, 137-38
Catlinite pipes, 93
Cattail mats, 77
Cayuga Indians, population of, 14
Cedar tree, 65
Central Algonkian tribes, 13-15
Ceremonies (ceremonial life), 85-93; (see also specific ceremonies, occasions, tribes); and folklore, 127-137; and games, 109-117; shamanism and cures, 95-106; tobacco ritual, 92, 93, and warfare, 48, 49
Charms, 98, 103-04, 121; child's, 30; hunting, 23
Cheekbones (malars), 15
Cherries, 21
Chibia'bos, 42, 43, 129, 130; defined, 139
Chicago, Indian name for, 12
Chief Dance, 88
Chiefs (chieftainship), 48; duties of, 48; and names (naming), 33; and rice harvesting, 26, 27; and warfare, 48
Children (childhood), 33-35, 37, 38; (see also Boys; Girls); birth and infancy, 15, 29-30, 32; games, 117; love of, 43; naming of, 32-33; personality patterns, 33, 34; puberty, 37-38; training of, 33-38
Chippewa (Ojibwa) Indians, 15; arrows, 61; bear ceremony, 91; canoes, 12; Chief Dance, 88; children, 33; clothing, 51-52, 55, 57; cradle boards, 30, 32; cup and pin game, 115-16; dancing 85-90, 124-25; death and burial, 40-43; dental pictographs, 66; dice game, 115; double ball game, 113; Drum Dance, 88-90; fishing, 21-2; hide preparation, 80-2; lacrosse, 109, 110, 112; medicine, 103-04; Medicine Dance, 85-88; moccasin game, 112; moccasins, 51, 52; mythology and folklore, 127-137; names, 32-3; population of, 13; and singing, 119, 121-22, 124-25; social organization, 45-49; and

warfare (scalping), 48-9; wild rice, 26-28
Chipped-stone artifacts, 16-17, 81
Chokecherries, 21
Christianity, 90-91; missionaries, 91; Native American Church, 90
Clairvoyant ability, shaman's, 95
Clans: folklore and, 128; membership in, 46-7
Climate, 11-12
Cloth goods, as game prizes, 110
Clothing, 51-2, 55, 57, 83; (see also specific items); decorating, 69, 72; gifts of, 125, hide preparation, 80-82; men's, 51-2, 55; offerings to spirits, 106; women's, 55, 57
Coiled basketry, 79, 139
Colonists, 14
Common-law marriage, 39
Communities, organization by, 45-47
Conestoga Indians, population, 14
Confederacies, organization into, 15
Coniferous trees, 11
Conjuror shamans, 95-6, 98, 101
Connecticut, Indian name for, 12
Containers, 11, 15, 21-2, 28, 66, 69, 79; birchbark, 15, 19-20; maple sugar, 19; metal, 19; woven, 74, 77
Cooking: corn, 20; fish, 22; meat, 25; rice, 27; vessels and containers, 19-20, 25, 66; (see also Containers)
Copperwork, 16, 83
Cord, bark-fiber, 21. See also Twine
Corn, 12, 19, 20-1, 62; meal from, 62; woven hulling bags, 77
"Coup" counting, 49
Courting (courtship), 34, 38-9; and marriage, 38-9; and music, 39, 119, 121
Cowrie shells, 86
Cradle boards, 30, 32
Cranberries, 21
Creation myth, 127, 129-30, 131-32
Cree Indians: population, 13; quillwork, 51, 69
Crooked knives, 139
Cross-cousin marriage, 38, 45
Cross Fire cult, 90
Culture heroes, 85, 127 ff. See also specific culture heroes
Cupping, 101-02
Cup and pin game, 115-16; equipment, 116; method of play, 116; scoring, 116
Cures (curing); beliefs and ceremonies, 86-88, 90, 109; shamanism and, 95-101; songs and, 119, 124

Dances (dancing), 119-125; Brave (Chief) Dance, 88; Drum (Dream) Dance, 40, 88-90, 119, 121-22, 124; Medicine Dance, 85-88, 119, 122, 124; and ricing, 27, 28; Scalp Dance, 124-25; War Dance, 32, 49, 88, 122, 124-25; Women's Dance, 122, 125

"Dancing the rice," 27

Deadfalls, 23, 25

Death (and the dead), 29, 40-42; burial and mourning, 40-42; disposition of (prehistory 17; funeral ceremony, 42; graves, 42-3; soul and spirits beliefs, 41-43

Debert site, Nova Scotia, 16

Decorative arts, 69-74 (see also Designs; specific items); beadwork, 51, 52, 55, 57, 69; leatherwork, 51; quillwork, 51, 52, 69; ribbonwork, 51, 52, 57, 74; silverwork, 83; weaving, 74

Deer (see also Deerskin): hunting of, 14, 23; preparation of hides, 80-82; use of hair of, 55

Deerskin (buckskin) clothing, 51-2, 55, 57

Delaware Indians, population of, 13

Densmore, Frances, 21, 28, 40, 103, 115, 116, 122, 125

Dental pictographs, 66

Designs, 69, 72; beadwork (embroidery 72; dental pictographs, 66; floral, 72, 74; geometric, 72, 74, 77; on lacrosse balls, 109; quillwork, 69; ribbonwork, 74; in weaving, 74; woodwork, 61; zoomorphic, 74, 77

Detroit Fort, 48

Dice game, 115; equipment for, 115; scoring in, 115

Disease(s), 12; music and, 119-125; shamanism and cures, 95-106. See also Cures

Doctors. See Shamans

Dogbane charm, 104

Dogs, 26; sacrifice and eating of, 49; taboos, 89, 98; toboggan-pulling, 62

Dogwood bark, 68

Dolichocephaly (longheadedness), 15

Dolls, 35

Dome-shaped wigwams, 14, 57; construction of, 57

Double ball game, 113

Drawings (mnemonic devices), 124

Dream (Drum) Dance, 40, 88-90, 119, 121, 122, 124

Dreams (dreaming), 32, 105, 106; and fasting, 37, 98, 104; fetishes, 104; and guardian spirits, 37; and Medicine Dance, 86, 119; and naming, 32; and songs, 119; vision quest, 34, 37, 91, 95, 119

Dresses, 55

Drills, 17

Drum (Dream) Dance, 40, 88-90, 119, 121, 122, 124

"Drum religion," 89

Drums (drumming), 28, 82, 119-120; Drum Dance, 40, 88-90, 119, 121, 122, 124; moccasin game, 112; in peyote religion, 91; shamans and, 95, 98; tambourine, 119-20; water, 119

Dual divisions (moieties), 47, 110, 140

Dugouts, 62

Dwellings, 57-59, (see also Tipis; Lodges; Wigwams); types of, 57-59

Dyes, use of, 52, 69

Eagle feathers, use of, 55, 61

Earth moieties, 47

Eastern Algonkian tribes (U.S.), 14; population of, 13

Eden site, 16

Effigy mounds, 17

Elbow pipes, 17

Elk hunting, 14

Elm tree, 11; wood, 61

Embroidery, bead, 51, 69; spot (overlay) stitch, 72

End scrapers, 16

English-American vocabulary, Indian additions to, 12; influence on Indian names, 33

Erie Indians, population of, 14

Erythema, 102

Ethical instruction, 89, 127

Europeans, contact with and influence of, 17, 38, 69, 72; see also Whites

Evil, shamanism and, 95, 96, 98, 103-06

Exogamy, 46-7

Extended family, 46

Eye color, Woodland Indians, 15

Family, the, 46; see also Life cycle; specific members

Farb, Peter, 11

Fasts (fasting); and dreams, 34, 37, 38, 104; and hunting, 23; at puberty, 37, 38

Father-son relationship, 33-4, 37

Feasts (feasting), 25; bear ceremony, 91; Brave Dance, 88; clan, 47; curative, 32; Drum Dance, 90; First Game, 25; for the dead, 42; Medicine Dance, 86; peyote religion, 91; puberty, 37; utensils, 61-2

Feathers, use of in arrow construction, 61; in headdress, 55

Fetishes: dream, 104; figurine, 51, 96

Fiber bark string (twine), 21, 66, 68

Figurine fetishes, 51, 96

Finger weaving, 77

Fire; and mourning ceremony, 42, 43; woodwork reduction by, 61

Fireplaces, 57

First Fruits or Game Offering, 20, 25

Fish (fishing), 14, 17, 19, 20, 21-2; catching, 21, 61; cooking, 22; lures, 21, 61

Flageolet, 121

Flagroot charm, 104

Flaked tools (flaking), 16, 17

Floral decorative designs, 72, 74

Flutes, 39, 119, 121

Folklore, 127-137

Food (food supply; diet), 11, 15; (see also Food quest; specific items); agriculture, 20; and the dead, 41, 43; fishing, 21-2; gardening, 20; gathering, 21; gifts and offerings, 20, 21, 38, 41, 42-3, 106; hunting and traping, 23, 25; (see also Hunting); maple sugar, 19-20; mealtime, 26; preparation (cooking), 20, 22, 25, 28; rice, 26-28

Food quest, 14, 15, 19-28; (see also Food); agriculture, 20; fishing, 21-2; gathering, 21; hunting and trapping, 23-25; maple sugar, 19-20; prehistoric, 17; wild ricing, 26-28

Foot races, 112

Forest Potawatomi, 15. See also Potawatomi

Forest tribes, 11-17 ff. See also specific tribes and aspects, e.g., Decorative arts; Hunting; Life cycle; Material culture; Religion

Four, religious significance of number, 91, 112

Fox hunting, 23

Fox Indians, 15; Black Hawk war, 48; decorative arts, 74; lacrosse, 110; moieties, 47; peyote religion, 90; population, 13; shamanism, 95; storytelling, 129

Fright; use in child-training of, 34;

role of "frightener," 34

Fruit(s), 11, 21; First Fruits Offering, 20, 25; puberty offerings, 38

Funeral ceremony, 40

Fur trading (fur traders), 65

Games, 109-117; children's, 117; cup and pin game, 115-16; dice, 115; double ball game, 113; guessing, 112; handgame, 113; lacrosse, 109-110; moccasin game, 112; snow snake, 116-17; wrestling and kicking, 112

Gardening, 11, 15, 17, 20

Garters, 69, 74, 77

Geese, in folklore, 134

Geometrical decorative designs, 72, 74, 77; "otter tail," 72

German silver, 51, 57, 83

Ghosts, belief in, 40, 85; dancing ghosts, 40

Giants, stories of, 128

Gifts (gift-giving and exchanges), 90, 93, 110, 115, 128; (see also specific kinds, e.g. Tobacco); child's, 30, 32; courtship, 39; in Drum Dance, 90; in Women's Dance, 125

Girls (see also Children; Women); childhood of, 37-8; and menstrual taboos, 37-8, 105; training of, 38; and wild ricing, 27

Glacial Kame culture, 16

Gooseberries, 21

Goose oil, 32

Gorgets, 16

Government (political organization), Woodland Indians, 14-15, 48

Grandparent-child relationship, 33, 46

Grass baskets, 79

Grass Dance, 89

Grass dolls, 37

Gravers (engraving tools), 16

Graves, 40-42; First Fruits Offering at, 20; markers, 41

Grease, 25, 32

Great Ancestral Bear clan, 47

Great Lakes region, 11-12, 15 (see also specific tribes); canoes, 65; fishing, 21-2; ribbonwork, 74

Great Spirit (Manido), 20. See also Manido

Guardian spirits, 32, 37, 85, 88, 105, 106

Guessing games, 112

Guns, bows replaced by, 23

Makuks (birchbark containers), 20, 21, 66, 139

Malecite Indians, population of, 13

Manabush (Nanabush), 42, 127, 133-34, 139

Manido (spirit; plural, *manidog),* 20, 139; folklore and stories of, 130-32, 134, 136; religious and ceremonialism and, 85-93, 109

Maple sugar, 19-20, 66; gathering of, 19-20; use of, 20; origin myth, 132

Maple trees, 11, 61. *See also* Maple sugar

Marquette, Father, 28

Marriage 38-39, 45-47; after mourning, 42; clan function in, 45, 47; cross-cousin, 38, 45; intermarriage with whites, 12, 33; levirate, 42; preparation of girls for, 34-5; sororate, 38; taboos, 42; weddings, 39

Massachuset Indians, population of, 13

Mascoutens, 15. *See also* Potawatomi

Massachusetts, Indian name of, 12

Material culture, 11, 14-15, 51-83; *(see also* specific aspects; items; people); prehistoric, 16-17

Mats; birchbark, 66, 77, 79; use in dwellings, 57, 58, 59; woven, 77, 79

Meat, cooking and preparation of, 25

Medicine Dance, 29, 45, 58, 85-88 *(see also* Midé'wiwin); degrees, 87; "shooting" of the shells, 87

Medicine Lodge Society, 85-8; lodge construction, 58, 86

Medicine men. *See* Priests; Shamans

Medicine(s), 11, 21, 34, 102-04; instruction in, 85, 86

Menomini Indians, 15; bear ceremony, 91; bows and arrows, 61; "catfish" snowshoes, 62; chiefs, 48; clans, 47; folklore, 127, 128, 133-34, 137-38; food, 20, 26-28; games, 109, 112-13, 116; moccasins, 52; "mouse corn," 20; peyote religion, 90; population of, 13; shamanism, 95, 96; warfare, 48, 49; wild ricing, 26-8

Menstruation, 26, 29; taboos, 26, 105; huts, 37-8, 58; origin folklore, 133

Mescal, use of, 90

Metalwork, 83

Mexico, 90, 110

Miami Indians, 15; clans, 47; decorative arts, 74; population of, 13

Michigan, Lake, Indian name for, 12

Michilimackinac, 112

Micmac Indians, population of, 13

Microcommunities, 46

Midé', 40, 41, 139; *(see also Midé'wiwin);* bag, 40

Midé'wiwin, 85-8, 89, 92, 102, 119, 121, 122, 124, 127, 129, 139; folklore, 127, 129; Medicine Dance, 29, 45, 58, 85-8, 92; music, 119, 120, 122, 124; priests, 38, 40-1, 86-7, 96; scrolls, 66

Mi'gis, 86, 87; definition of, 140

Milkweed, in diet, 21

Milkwort charm, 104

Milwaukee, Indian name for, 12

Missionaries, 91

Mississippi River, Indian name for, 12

Moccasin game, 112-13

Moccasins, 12, 27, 29, 51-2, 55, 57; flaps, 52; manufacture of, 52; styles, 52; vamps, 52

Mohawk Indians, population of, 14

Moiety, 47, 110; defined, 140

Mongoloid traits, Woodland Indians, 15

Montagnais, 11, 14, 15; population of, 13

Montauk Indians, population of, 13

Moon, beliefs and folklore, 85, 137

Moose, 15, 23, 55, 66

Moosecalls, birchbark, 66

Morning Star, 95

Mortars and pestles, 62

Mother-child relationship, 29-30, 32, 33-35, 37

Mother-in-law taboo, 39

Mound building, 16, 17

Mourning, 40-43; removal ceremony, 42, 105; taboos, 105

Multifamily long houses, 14

Music, 119-125, *(see also* Dances [dancing]; Songs [singing])

Musical instruments, 119, 121

Muški'ki, defined, 140

Myths (mythology), 127-138

Names (naming); children, 32-3, 47; clans and, 47; geographical, 12; namesake names, 33; nicknames, 33

Narragansett Indians, 15; population of, 13

Naskapi Indians, 11, 14; population of, 13; roundheadedness in, 15

Native American Church, 90

Necklaces, 69

Needles, mat-weaving, 79

Nets, fishing, 21, 22

Nettle-stalk fiber, 21, 25

Nokomis, 132

Nuts, in diet, 11, 20, 21

"Offering tree," 106
Ojibwa, *See* Chippewa
Old age, 40; death, burial, and mourning, 40-43
Old Copper culture, 16
Omaha Indians; Grass Dance, 88-9; kinship system, 45
Oneida Indians; baskets, 79; population of, 14
Onions, in diet, 21
Onondaga Indians, population of, 14
Ontario, Lake, Indian name for, 12
Oshkosh, Chief, 33
Ottawa Indians, 15; bear ceremony, 91; *Manabush* myth, 127; population of, 13
Otter; medicine bag, 119; skin turbans, 52, 55
Owls; children's fear of, 34; owl mask, 34

Paddles, canoe, 65
Painting, facial, death and burial (Chippewa), 40, 43
Paleo-Indians, 16
Paper birch, use of, 11
Paralysis, shamanism and, 105
Parent-children relationship, 29-30, 32-35, 37, 38, 46
Patrilineal clans, 14
Peace (calumet) pipe, 89, 92-3
Peace treaties, smoking and, 92
Peaked lodge, 58
Pennacook Indians, population of, 13
Peoria Indians, population of, 13
Pequot Indians, population of, 13
Percussion flaking, 17
Pestles, 62
Peyote religion, 90-1, 140; society, 40, 90-1; spineless cactus mescal *(Lophophora williamsii)*, 90
Phratries, 47
Physical types, Woodland Indians, 15-16
Piankashaw Indians, population of, 13
Pine needles, dolls made of, 37
Pipes, tobacco, 92-3; decorative work on pipe stems, 69, 83; elbow, 17; tube, 16
Pitfalls, 23
Plains Indians (*see also* specific tribes); clothing, 52; peyote religion, 90-1; warfare, 49
Plants (plant life), 11-12 (*see also* specific kinds); food gathering, 21, 34; use of fibers of, 11
Playthings. *See* Toys

Pleistocene period, 16
Plum stones (game and equipment), 115
Points (spear points), 16; fluted, 16; nonfluted, 16
Policemen (policing function); 27, 47, 48
Political structure, Woodland Indians, 14-15, 48
Polygyny (and monogamy), 38
Pontiac, Chief, uprisings led by, 48, 112
Popcorn, 20
Population statistics, Woodland Indians, 12-14
Porcupine, hair, use of, 55; quillwork, 69
Potatoes, in diet, 21
Potawatomi Indians, 15; bear ceremony, 91; chiefs, 48; children, 33, 37; courtship, 39; death and burial, 42; decorative arts, 74; games, 110, 113, 115; mythology, 129; peyote religion, 90; population of 13; pregnancy taboos, 29; puberty, 37
Pottery, 16, 17, 51
Pouches, umbilical cord, 29, 30
Powwow, the, 88. *See also* Drum (Dream) Dance
Prairie Potawatomi (Mascouten), 15 (*see also* Potawatomi); population of, 13
Prairie tribes, 11-7 ff. *See also* specific tribes and aspects, e.g. Decorative arts; Food; Life cycle; Religion
Prairie wolves, 23
Pregnancy, 29-30
Prehistory, Woodland Indians, 16-17
Priests, 48, 85-7 (*see also* Shamanism; specific ceremonies and societies); and Medicine Dance, 87, 88, 89, 90
Prizes, games and, 109, 110, 113, 115
Prophecy, dreams and, 37
Protective (preventive) medicine, 103-06
Puberty; fasting, 32, 34, 37-8, 105; vision quest and, 37-8
Pumpkins, 12
Puppets, used by shamans of, 96

Quillwork, 69, 72

Rabbits, taboos, 29
Rackets, lacrosse, 109
Radin, Paul, 38, 39, 47
Radiocarbon dating, 16
Raids (raiding), 48-9
Raspberries, 21
Rattles, 119, 121
Red Ocher culture, 16

Relationships, interpersonal, 45-7

Religion (religious concepts and ceremonial life), 14, 85-93; Bear ceremonialism, 91; Brave (Chief) Dance, 88; Drum (War) Dance, 88-90; folklore, 127-137; games and, 109-117; Medicine Dance, 85-8; music and, 119-125; peyote, 90; shamanism and cures, 95-106

Residence patterns, 46, 58; marriage and, 40, 46

Respect, kinship relationships and, 46

"Restoring the mourners," ceremony, 43

Ribbonwork (silk appliqué), 51, 52, 55, 57, 74; blind stitch, 74; cross-stitch, 74

Rice, 20, 26-8; wild ricing, 26-8

Roach (animal hair headdress), 55

Road of souls, 40, 42

Robes, buckskin, 52

Roe, sturgeon, 22

"Round dance," 125

Roundheadedness, 15

Runner, defined, 140

Sacred bundles, 47

Sacred drums, 88-90

Sacred objects (ishiu'winen), 32, 104, 140

Sacrifices (sacrificing); and hunting, 23; of rice, 26; and warfare, 49

Sashes, 55-6; weaving of, 77

Sauk Indians, 13, 15; headdress, 55; lacrosse, 110; peyote religion, 90; ribbonwork, 74; storytelling, 129; warfare, 48

Scalp Dance, 49, 124-5

Scalping, 49, 124

Scalp lock, as headdress, 55

Scalp poles, 49, 124

Scottsbluff site, 16

Scrapers, 16, 17, 80-2

Sculpture, 51

Seines, fishing, 21-2

Seneca Indians, population of, 6

Seneca snakeroot charm, 104

Settlements, 45

Shamans (shamanism), 20-1, 48, 85-6; and curing, 95-6; defined, 140

Shawnee Indians, 15; population of, 13

Sickness (health); games and, 109; religious ceremonies and, 85, 86-7, 88, 90-1; shamanism and curative techniques, 95-106

Silk appliqué (ribbonwork), 51, 52, 55, 57, 74; blind stitch, 74; cross-stitch, 74

Silverwork, 51, 57, 83; German silver, 51, 57, 83

Siouan (calumet) pipe, 92

Sioux, the, 89; language 15

Skin color, Woodland Indians, 15

Skinner, Alanson, 15, 26, 27, 39, 42, 48, 74, 79, 96, 110, 119, 128, 129

Skirts, 55

Sky moiety, 47

Slavery, 46

Sleds, 62

Sleeping arrangements, 57-8

Smoking (see also Tobacco); hide preparation and, 82; powdered-root hunting charms, 23, 92;

Snakes, flagroot charm against, 104

Snowshoes, 12, 14; "bear paw," 62; catfish, 62; construction of, 62

Snow snake game, 116-17

Soap, manufacture of, 25

Social organization, 14-15, 45-9; "atomistic," 45; clans 46-7; dual division (moieties), 47; government, 48; kinship 45-7

Songs (singing), 49, 119-125; Drum (Dream) Dance, 40, 89-90, 119, 122, 124; Medicine Dance, 86; Midé society, 121-22, 124; moccasin game, 112; personality and voice styles, 121-22; peyote religion, 90-1; rhythm, 121-22; Scalp Dance, 124-25; War Dance, 88, 122, 125

Sorcery, 96, 98

Sororate marriage, 38

Soul, beliefs and magic practices, 40-43, 98, 101

Spears, 61; fishing, 21-2; points, 16

Sphagnum moss, 30

Spirit bundles, 43

Spirits and the spirit world (manido, manidog), 20, 29, 32, 37, 85-93, 140; music and, 119-125; religion and ceremonial life and, 85, 95, 109; and shamanism and curing, 95-107; Underneath, 26

Splint baskets, 79

Spoons, 61-2; handles, 61

Squash, 12, 19

Stockaded villages, use of, 14

Stockbridge Indians, baskets of, 79

Stone, use of, 11, 16-17, 58

Storage bags, weaving of, 74

Stories and story-telling, 127-137

Storms, 85, 88, 104

Straw man, use in sympathetic magic of, 105

Stretching frames, 81-2

Weapons, 19. *See also* specific kinds, uses

Weaving, 74, 77; checkerwork, 77; designs, 74, 77; embroidery, 69, 72, 74 finger, 77; mats, 77, 79; netting and braiding, 77; over-and-under, 77; warp and weft, 74, 140

Wɛ'ɛ, 32, 140

Wenebojo, 42, 85, 92, 140; and creation of the world, 131; Dancing Geese story and, 134-35; and origin of maple sugar, 132; stories of, 129-132; and the Wolves (story), 129

Whistles, 119

Whitebirch zone, 65

Whites, the, 12, 14, 17, 19, 89 (*see also* Europeans; specific countries, e.g., U.S. Government); Indian games and, 113; Indian wars with, 15, 48; intermarriage with Indians, 12, 33

Wicker baskets, 79

Widows, 43

Wigwams, 11, 20, 57-9, 79; construction of, 57-9; death and burial, 41; domeshaped, 15, 57; shamans and use of, 96, 102

Wild food, gathering of, 21. *See also* specific kinds

Wild rice (wild ricing), 26-8; harvesting, 26; husking, 27; preparing, 27, 28; serving, 28; winnowing, 27

Windigo, 85, 128, 135-37, 140

Winds (windstorms), beliefs and practices, 85, 104

Winnebago Indians, 12, 15; baskets, 79; "catfish" snowshoes, 62; clans, 47; corn, 20; fasts and guardian spirits, 37; games, 112; government, 48; menstrual taboos, 38; moccasins, 52; mother-in-law taboo, 39; mythology, 128; origin of, 17; and peyote religion, 90; population of 13; pregnancy taboos, 29; and scalping, 49

Winnowing process, rice, 27

Wisconsin, 12, 15, 17, 65, 68

Wi'ske, 42, 140

Wolf clan, 46

Wolves; hunting of, 23; and *Wenebojo* (story), 129-31

Women (*see also* Girls); childhood and pregnancy, 29-30; 33-4; clothing, 55-7; courtship and marriage, 38-9; cupping done by, 101; decorative arts, 51, 69, 72, 74, 77, 79 (*see also* Beadwork; Leatherwork; Weaving); and Drum Dance, 89; and fishing, 21-2; food gathering, 21; and games, 109, 113, 115-16; hair styles, 57; height, 16; hide preparation, 79-82; menstruation taboos, 26, 29, 37-8, 105; mother-child relationship, 29-30, 32, 33-5; mourning and re-marriage, 42-3; and ricing, 26-8; story of origin of menstruation in, 133; tattooing done by, 102

Women's Dance, 122, 125

Woods and bark, use of, 11, 61-2, 65-6, 68. *See also* specific items, uses

Woodwork, 61-2

Wrestling, 112

Yarn (bags, sashes, garters), 74, 77

Youth's Dance, 25